Letters
to
America

THE WORLD

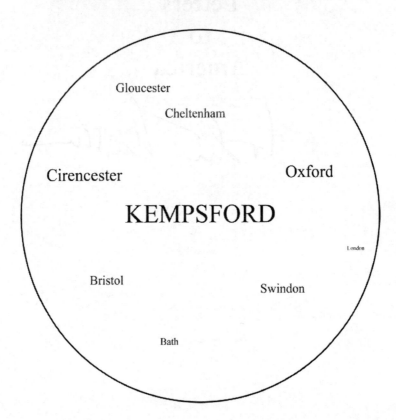

Letters
to
America

A Year in the Cotswolds

Vicki Weissman

Copyright © 2010 by Vicki Weissman

All rights reserved. No part of this publication may be reproduced or
transmitted in any form or by any means, electronic or mechanical
including photocopying, recording or any information storage or
retrieval system, without prior permission in writing from the publisher.

The right of Vicki Weissman to be identified as the author of this work
has been asserted by her in accordance with the Copyright, Designs and
Patents Act 1988.

First published in the United Kingdom in 2010
by Frederica Freer Publishing

ISBN 978-0-9563798-1-8

Produced by
The Choir Press, Gloucester
www.thechoirpress.co.uk

Contents

Acknowledgements

I must thank the following friends and colleagues. Some for their kindness, some for their skills and one for his patience!

To Frederica Freer, a noble editor and publisher, I owe the exemplary accuracy of this text. Miles Bailey, printer extraordinaire, is wholly responsible for the clarity and distinction of the book's final form. Susan Keeble, a neighbour and friend, produced the delightful line drawings which enliven several of the pieces and last, but by no means least, Alasdair Kirk, and the team at Designtoo. Alasdair took my photograph (flattering indeed) while Dan and Mark helped hugely with making sure that photographs and drawings were with Miles Bailey on the dot of the deadline.

Two others must be thanked – with love. First of all Stephen Kaye, Editor and owner of *The Millbrook Independent*. Had he not had the courage to plunge into the murky waters of newspaper production these columns would never have been written. And he took the gamble that his readers would enjoy news from afar. The last person to whom thanks are imperative is my husband, Steve. Every Sunday evening he has had a terrible supper because my mind has been on higher things. He has put up with it.

I married a saint.

Vicki Weissman
Kempsford
November, 2010

Prologue

Early in 2009 an old friend in America decided it was time to push the boat out. His local newspaper in upstate New York had folded. He felt, and his wife agreed, that such papers are the lifeblood of small communities. So with great courage and no small trepidation he became a publisher – and *The Millbrook Independent* is the result.

I thought he might like some support and offered to send him a weekly piece. So now *The Millbrook Independent* is the only newspaper in North America to carry a regular piece from the English heartland. It seems it goes down pretty well with the readers.

I love doing it. For a start it is a weekly workout for my ageing brain, but even more fun is finding something to write about. It is easy to float along thinking how agreeable country life is and how pleasant the village. But vaguely appreciative pieces quickly become dull, so every week I have had to focus on the minutiae, to find something properly local as a worthwhile topic. I now know much more about my neighbourhood and, I like to think, much more about how things actually work around here.

Quite when and how the idea of making this collection popped up I can't really remember. Partly I just wanted to see a year's work in one bundle, but also I hoped that people might find it entertaining to read reflections on a year of Cotswold events written with a mostly loving eye. There was only one way to find out. So *Letters to America: A Year in the Cotswolds* was born. I hope I was right and that reading through these pieces proves as enjoyable for you as writing them was for me.

For
SDW

I

Kempsford and Millbrook

10 November 2009

A long-standing friendship between the editor of *The Mill-brook Independent*'s family and your Kempsford correspondent may be a slim enough connection between our village and yours, but, despite the width of the Atlantic, our communities may, in fact, have quite a lot in common. So we decided to give it a go.

This is a rural world. There are sheep all over the place and fields, either fallow, set-aside or planted up for next year's crop. You have to have a car to do your marketing. No shops in the village and the nearest decent supermarket is fifteen miles away. People get exercised over development – which usually means horrible houses not in keeping – local history, wetlands and their preservation, gardening (Big Time) and, this being serious horse country, hunting, still pursuable within the law by an intelligent MFH, Pony Club, dressage and tack sales. They also have views on more arcane matters such as the proper way to keep bantams, whether chickens should be allowed the run of the garden or be penned, how should tomatoes be fed, what is the best way to raise, kill and cook a goose and what do you do with rogue fowl? For us this last became a burning issue when our peacocks ate the neighbours' cabbage. These were birds who loved to party –

when there was a wedding they would parade down the aisle with the bride – but in the end village pros and cons counted for nothing, the fox ate the lot of them. We were really sad at the loss of our fine-feathered companions who would stroll through the house and eat from our hands.

Today I am trying to figure out what to do with twenty rose bushes ordered on a whim because it was such a good offer, to position a new hedge and decide where and whether to put mole-traps. My husband, a Harvard man to his bootstraps, does not wish to be consulted. One ride on the new lawn-tractor, which promptly blew up with him on board, has convinced him that gardening and all related matters are an Englishwoman's work.

This is also a day of connection for the country as a whole. The Remembrance Day service for the dead of both World Wars took place this morning. The Queen, at advanced years, laid a wreath at the national memorial, The Cenotaph, and walked backwards, down steps. Shall I be able to do that when I'm in my eighties?

For this village today is especially poignant. Five minutes up the road is Fairford Air Base. Since World War II this has been a base for US troops as well as our own. Today we remembered not just the great World Wars but also those much nearer our time and those which still continue, with our troops and yours. The boy who comes to do the rubbish and clean the boots on Saturday morning goes to bowling on the base on Saturday afternoon. His girlfriend is there too. And USAF children attend our village Primary School. So there is a connection between Millbrook and us – I think it will be fun to explore it.

II

Ribbons and Roses

17 November 2009

I don't know what it is like in Millbrook, but here, were the Witch-finder General still to be in business, he'd be run off his feet. Wild-eyed women roam the streets, muttering and clutching little bits of paper, with holly in their baskets and ivy leaves trailing. Occasionally they stop – and, with a cry of triumph – strike out an item on their paper with a sharp-pointed pencil. But this is no satanic ritual, rather the annual hysteria which marks the birth of Our Lord.

I too have succumbed. In this past week I have demanded a pair of scissors from a supervisor and, irritated beyond patience by computer nit-picking, chopped my store card, my friend for the last forty years, into tiny pieces before her baffled eyes. Clearly she thought I was crazy, but my goodness, did I feel better. And in the local small post office – oh rural trial – waiting in line while those lucky souls who had made it to the counter discussed at length whether or not they needed a receipt, whether the parcel would have to be signed for, before segueing into an anecdote about their dog and the frost, I did at one point ask rather loudly, "Is this a Post Office or a Counselling Service?"

It's no better at home. In room after room there are little heaps of bows, ribbons, Scotch tape and Christmas wrapping and on the library table a mountain of cards waiting for the annual message. Not a lot of tasty dinners are being served at present, but there are plenty of empty wine bottles to go to the dump. My husband glues himself to the TV and the chess tournament and waits for it all to be over.

But there is one wonderful break in the clouds. The bare-root roses have arrived. When I can no longer bear to try to decide who shall have what and from whom I slip into another fine company. Where should Lady Emma Hamilton go? Will she do well with Gertrude Jekyll? Or perhaps she and Grace might settle down nicely together. Then there's Jubilee Celebration to be placed and the Alnwick Rose. And what about Port Sunlight? There is also the question of Spirit of Freedom and The Mayflower – bought in memory of a dear New York friend who died earlier this year. Should they mingle in with their English cousins, or have an American corner of their own?

I have the shape of the new beds drawn out and a little chart of the expected size of the bushes when they are full grown. Never a woman for maths I nonetheless find it very soothing indeed to be working out this placement. Should I follow the golden rule, three of the same clutched together? Or shall I just randomly mix and mingle these glorious shades of apricot and pink?

After about an hour or so of this my brain is quite rested and I can go back to the maelstrom that is Christmas. And contemplate the extraordinary fact that, come the summer, these bare-rooted spiky bundles will be profuse in bloom and scent. Birth and re-birth, on it goes. The country life can drive you nuts occasionally, but, oh, the consolations!

III

The Dog-Fox and the Downturn

24 November 2009

A raw and blustery day. And Christmas is coming – with all that that implies for the pocket. So a word much batted about is "recession". Or at least much batted in the national newspapers, headlines heated to boiling point by the Dubai debacle. Oddly enough, despite dire predictions of a total slump in retail trade, with many supporting graphs to prove it, there's not much evidence of gloom here in Kempsford. The only person I know whose income has taken a tumble is James, whose family lives in a fine house at the other end of the village and who, every week, supplies six delicious eggs from his little flock of Marans, Old Speckleds and what he calls Profiteroles. In return I give him £1 and last week's empty egg-box. But it's not recession – his hens have just stopped laying till the weather warms up. The usual goodly number of cars stands outside the pub and the Primary School Christmas Grotto was doing brisk business on Saturday morning. Christmas lights are going up and Christmas drinks invitations circulating. It seems a small village is not a bad place to be when economic chill strikes.

But a few days ago I got quite another view of the

situation. My neighbour and I have reached agreement over his sycamore trees. They shade my vegetable garden. So I will pay to have them lopped and he will get the firewood. As our yews needed trimming I called in the tree surgeon. A highly qualified young man showed up, with permission from Cotswold District Council to proceed. With chainsaw, chipper and assistant he was ready for a couple of days' work.

But Nature intervened. In gale-force wind he could not do the really big limbs. I was afraid for his life and he was afraid for my greenhouse roof. So we agreed he'd finish off another day. "Don't worry if you can't come till Easter," I said cheerfully. "We shan't be planting veg before that." "Oh," he said, "if we leave it that long I could be out of business." So I asked him about this. In the last month two cancellations, several non-follow ups and one £50,000 job on indefinite hold. "Much tree work is non-essential – it's the first thing to go." he explained. And this was a chap in his early forties, with a wife and four children to support. Later that week I asked one of my garden helpers how he was doing. "Slowing down, definitely slowing down," he told me. "People wanted all the hours I could spare before, but they're not so keen now." So even round here, where houses are large and gardens larger, the thin end of the wedge has made its appearance.

As I say, you wouldn't notice it – and everyone will get on with it. For some in the rural world there's even a benefit. Local beaters are doing even better than usual when they sell on their partridge and pheasant. Craft markets are busy, their nice things are cheaper than Harrods. I'm waiting for a call from a friend who every year comes to cut our hollies to make Christmas wreaths. They are exquisite and she always sells her work. (As I am the holly source mine is a present, lucky me!) But she is anxious and will probably make fewer this year. Neighbourhood restaurants have simplified their menus and our local taxi reports not so many people needing a ride home after a bibulous dinner out. But one thing you can be sure of, we won't make national news. It's only the countryside, no factory closures here.

An old dog fox has just lollopped his way over the terrace. It's broad daylight and he's really close to the house. Maybe dustbin yields are down? I'm not saying it's time to draw the covered wagons into a circle, but perhaps we should be remembering how to do it!

IV

A Record and a Thanksgiving

1 December 2009

Saturday, 21 November, was a foul night. Blowing a gale and pouring with rain. Anyone with a half a brain would have been settled cosily by the fire. Not however the case in this house. Instead we drove thirty-five minutes up single-track Cotswold lanes to the tiny village of Caudle Green. The reason? A book launch. But for a book rather different from usual. Gerald Stewart, the author, is eighty-four years old. He has lived his entire life here in Gloucestershire, within ten miles of where he was born. Apart from war service he has not left the UK. He was a roof tiler and then a gardener. And that is where the book comes in.

The garden he has worked on for the last fifty years belonged to one of the famous Mitford sisters – Pamela – who became Pamela Jackson. On her death Mrs Jackson left her house to one of her nieces, the daughter of the present Dowager Duchess of Devonshire – the famously beautiful and witty Debo. Currently it is let to the niece's old friend, who is married to a distinguished botanical writer. She was chatting one day with Gerald, still the gardener, when he told her he had written the story of his life, in long-hand, for his grandchildren, Stephen and Emily. She asked to read it. And thought it so good it should be published. Funding was sought and found and the Dowager Duchess wrote a Foreword. This seemed like a book worth getting through the storm for.

And so it proved. *Pipe Lids and Hedgehogs: A Life in the Cotswolds and a War Abroad* evokes a world so long gone it is almost a fairy tale. Children wander freely through woods and fields, small boys stoke up the Vicarage boiler and pump the church organ to earn sixpence. A lady carrier takes her cart to Cirencester once a week, delivering for some and acquiring necessities for others. And helping her is young Gerald, who is parked in the pub corner with a lemonade while she and her pals have a glass of stout, some bread and cheese and a pinch of snuff.

His report of his War Years is extraordinary. With complete simplicity he describes just what is was like for a country lad called on to do his duty, "Here we dug in at a place called Elst, where I spent my twentieth birthday. This concludes the first quarter of my life". Great stylists have written about war. Gerald is no stylist, but a plain-spoken man remembering with perfect clarity what happened. The result is, as the Dowager Duchess says, "as chilling to the reader as it must have been for him". We tend to romanticize the countryside past, making it all haywains and beribboned bonny girls. As this little book makes clear it wasn't quite like that. But what shines through is a true love and knowledge of the land. And of contentment with a life well-lived and fulfilled within so small a radius. Well worth our stormy journey.

For you in Millbrook Thanksgiving has come and gone – we give thanks to be spared the torture of having to face not one but two turkeys in the space of a month! But having children and grandchildren in the US we are always aware of the Great Day. Gerald Stewart's little book is itself a thanksgiving for a life well-lived. And the Dowager Duchess's Foreword is a thanksgiving too, for a man whose constancy has enriched her family's life.

V

Christmas Giving – The Three Kings and The Rest of Us

22 December 2009

It's countdown time. Only four days to go and Christmas Day will be upon us. Retail figures for gift shopping are not as bad as expected and the usual mammoth spend-up on turkey, stuffing, brandy butter, mince-pies, Brussels sprouts, Christmas pudding, etcetera, etcetera, etcetera means you are quite likely to lose the will to live in the check-out queue. Consumerism survives!

But there is another side. This is an area rich in churches of great antiquity – my own records its first Vicar in the 800s and its great tower was erected in the 14th century. For most of the year however, apart from Easter Sunday and Harvest Festival, there is scant enthusiasm for attendance at any of them. But some visceral response to the Christmas story and its significance even in this predominantly secular age means that congregations will swell for this great festival. Between 17 December until Christmas Eve this tiny village will have celebrated seven different Christmas related events – carol services, crib services, carol singing at the pub, midnight mass – and on Christmas Day there are to be three communion services. Over the country as a whole three million are expected to attend Church of

England Christmas services and, when added together, those attending services of other denominations will reach a similar figure. That is three times the usual Sunday attendance. The King's College Carol Service of Nine Lessons and Carols was, as usual, heard worldwide and the Queen's Annual Christmas television broadcast will be watched globally. So what is it that moves us all?

It's not the weather – freezing cold it may well be in this hemisphere, accentuating the need to party, but down there in Australia my youngest sister and others of our friends are very warm indeed. Yet they will be celebrating and singing carols and opening presents just the same. It's not even down to colonial heritage – you in America gave us the old heave-ho a long time back and you are still at it!

Is it perhaps the story? Two people of low estate must go and take part in a census. Everybody is on the move to check in with the authorities. Not a room to be had anywhere. So bang, in the stable, short straw and nowhere for the wife to have her baby except a manger. Grim. So far so familiar these days, with all we read of deprivation and misery for refugees, for the poor, for all those affected by the many ways our world has found to inflict misery. But then, magically, first of all come witnesses, the shepherds, and then the kings with their gifts.

Whatever else we may or may not do as was done then at Bethlehem, we still do the gifts. The Salvation Army here pulls in huge sums for its lost souls, Crisis at Christmas will feed the homeless throughout London, Chedworth church, near here, has collected for Maggie's Cotswolds Cancer Centre, Home Start, another Cotswold charity, has done well and all over this area carol singers are out raising funds for countless other local and national charities. Collections at services are always generous and will go to all manner of needy causes. People may well be wondering if they can get away with a slightly less fancy token of esteem for their nearest and dearest, but they don't hesitate to put their hands in their pockets when asked to help truly shocking want.

So I guess we should all take heart. Christian, non-believer, uncommitted but loving to belt out a carol – there is something in the air on 25 December which, for just a brief moment, makes us think not just of the feast, but of all those who are without home and hearth and the comfort that that implies. We are lucky to have inherited such a tradition. Long may it continue.

From Kempsford to Millbrook – a Very Merry Christmas.

VI

The Boxing Day Hunt – and Why Not?

29 December 2009

Boxing Day is one of those English traditions that has not crossed the pond. 26 December used to be the day when the postman, the dustman, the newspaper-boy and other similarly vital helpers would call for their tip, or, as it was known, their Christmas Box. It certainly was still customary when I was a child. Nowadays most people have passed over their grateful envelope in the run-up to Christmas Day. But the name has stuck and Boxing Day remains a national holiday.

In the countryside it has one other tradition, the Boxing Day Meet. And, despite the Hunting Ban of 2004, over three hundred hunts are expected to gather this year. The origins of this custom are lost in the mists of time, but it remains an unshaken ceremonial. It has a slightly different flavour from the usual meet – frequently the hunt will gather at someone's house, rather than where there is a fair chance of an immediate chase. The good-looking younger members will make the most of a striking photo-opportunity and many proud grandpas will make sure that little Tommy or Emma is snapped on their pony beside his own enormous horse. And the consequent photo will be next year's family Christmas card. It is all a little less serious than usual and the pink coats, the stirrup cup and a touch of frost in the air make a healthy contrast to the terrible over-eating of the previous day.

But how, five years after the legislation, are these aficionados getting away with it? Partly because in rural areas there is a rather less dogmatic attitude to both animals and class. But also because the law does not prohibit running hounds on artificial trails and, once underway, these trails seldom fail to set up an actual fox. Even if such a fox is caught and killed the defence of lack of intention usually holds good. Of the nine prosecutions to reach court since 2004 only three have resulted in convictions.

So Boxing Day remains an occasion for those on both sides of the argument to lobby further for their cause. The Countryside Alliance hopes to demonstrate that the law as it stands is unworkable and should therefore either be repealed, or subject to a free vote by the next government. The Hunt Saboteurs Association will be focusing on current loopholes and pressing for clarification and tightening of the existing Act.

However the majority of the population will not really take much notice. I guess I am among their number. I have been to Boxing Day meets and found them both strikingly beautiful and slightly silly. On the whole grown-ups, in my opinion, could probably find something better to do with their time. And the only things I know about horses fit nicely on a very small piece of paper – i.e. a betting-slip. But if that is their idea of fun, let them get on with it. It is also true that the fox is not a nice animal. My chickens had to be penned up nightly or they would have been ripped to bits by a predator who was not even hungry. And our fine

peacock, Xerxes, came to a sad and savage end thanks to
Mr Reynard.

As our political parties gear-up for the next election both
the Tories and New Labour are making much of our stub-
born class divide and it is true that in the hunting world class
was once a big factor. Not many of the lower-orders were out
there tally-hoing, although the hunt definitely created a
substantial amount of country employment. Molly Keane's
novels, set in pre-war Ireland, are an unsurpassed record of
the bond between huntsmen, hunt-servants, horses, hounds,
farriers, blacksmiths and the like. But that's not the case now.
Yes, many of those riding to hounds are still from old county
families, but equally there are others out in the field who see
the chase and the gallop as a blissful escape from their daily
grind. A rather racy plumber in our village loved to get up
and away with the VWH (The Vale of the White Horse)
whose Boxing Day Meet drew a crowd of 6,000 supporters
at Cirencester Park, ancestral home of the Earls of Bathurst.
The Countryside Alliance has great hopes of these crowds
obliging a new Parliament to vote again on the current
banning legislation.

So no doubt, whoever wins the election, the Boxing Day
Hunt will be happening next year. And the year after that.
Our Environment Secretary says the debate is "about what
we think a decent civilized society should stand for". If
that's what he's after then I think on the whole we'd do
better to be worrying about man's inhumanity to man.

So tally-ho folks.

VII

The Big Freeze

5 January 2010

New Year has come and gone with all its proper rituals – parties, dances, Her Majesty's Honours List, plunges in Trafalgar Square's fountains – observed. These events usually generate enough gossip to get us comfortably through January. But this time all has been overtaken by the Big Freeze. We have had the coldest start to January for over thirty years and things show no sign of letting up. More snow is promised overnight and probably tomorrow. The UK is covered in the white stuff. The national dailies carry endless reports of valiant struggles through snowdrifts and indeed of one birth in the back of the car en route to the hospital. Television news loves it – newscasters get to fly in helicopters, over snowed-up roads and distant hamlets cut off from civilization. Dramatic picture follows dramatic picture.

But what of life down on the ground? The principal drawback here in Kempsford is that there is no shop. For the first two days, without a 4x4, you were stuck. If you were not munching through the Christmas leftovers, supplies became a concern. Then our central road was cleared and travel possible, albeit at a cautious speed. But lesser roads have not been touched and each night they have frozen over harder than ever. So you have to get to a pick-up point from whence kind neighbours will ferry you round. Our car has not been out since the first flakes – we can't get it out of the garage and down the drive. Having both a full freezer and a well-stocked cellar life chez-nous cannot be considered testing. I had to go round the garden with a broom taking snow off the most tender plants, as well as pushing it off the greenhouse roof which looked as though it was about to cave in. Hardly hardship.

But it was me in the mink up the ladder because people who come to work for us can't get here. And if they can't get to us they can't get to their other slots, so they are losing their weekly wage. Shoppers stay home for all but essentials, so retail sales plummet. It has been estimated that the cost to the national economy is in the region of £600 million per day. Farmers can't get Brussels sprouts out of the frozen ground, nor sugar-beet, cauliflowers are turned to mush and across the country some 6,000 acres of potatoes remain un-harvested, as well as carrots and parsnips. There is also the problem of getting supplementary feed to livestock. The National Farmers' Union and the RSPCA have opened an emergency hotline for calls from worried farmers.

I well remember East Coast winters, but your army of snow-ploughs came out and made roads passable in conditions far worse than these. Airplanes came and went pretty much on schedule, schools were seldom closed. That's because you are used to it. IT IS NOT SUPPOSED TO HAPPEN HERE! Currently, calls for snow-ploughs, grit and salt in all villages are loud and long, but for that to be put in place local taxes would have to rocket up. And then would come the outcry, "Unnecessary – only happens once in a blue moon".

So we shall just have to get on with it. It is a beautiful emptiness, the white covering swallowing sound. Tracks on the lawn are of deer, fox and badger. Right by the kitchen windows is a pyracantha and fieldfares have stripped it bare of berries. Having such reclusive birds in plain sight is a joy. There is another blessing. Bang goes the post-Christmas diet. When it's perishing cold you need hearty food – porridge, braised hare, mutton and dumplings – and probably a whiskey and water as a nightcap. So it's an unusual but not entirely unhappy New Year!

May we all enjoy a healthy and happy 2010.

VIII

The Big Thaw

12 January 2010

One thing's for sure – when you're in the middle of nowhere and a lot of white stuff comes out of the sky, you hunker down. Heat on, fires blazing, rugs and feet on the sofa and, apart from filling up the bird-feeders, no going outside! This has been the position here for the last ten days.

As a result, one reads more. But these days reading more isn't just a question of reaching for the good fat book you've been meaning to start on for the past few months – it also covers more poking around on the internet, just to check out some of the things you've had in the back of your mind lately. For me this produced a happy coincidence.

Having a good look through the many Millbrook NY sites, I found out all about the Nine Partners Friends Meeting House, seemingly Millbrook's most distinguished building. I had not known before that in 1745 there was a community of Friends big enough to build a log house for meetings, nor indeed that in 1780 a sufficiently wealthy like-minded group was in place to build the present Meeting House of fine brick – "The bricks are known to be particularly hard and weather resistant" notes Wikipedia – the original construction having been destroyed by fire in 1778.

So far so resolutely part of the usual early history of the Eastern seaboard.

But then came the surprise and the pleasing link. Reading *A Gambling Man*, a delightful new biography of Charles II*, I found that when Charles returned as king, despite his wishing to be, on the whole, lenient to those groups who had chopped off his father's head, he could not pull off this conciliatory manoeuvre. The be-headers had been dissenters, hot and strong – and Charles's Parliament, essentially Royalist, did not like them. So in 1665 The Five Mile Act was passed, forbidding free thinking ministers from coming within five miles of their former parishes. Two areas which would have no truck with this Act were Gloucester and Bristol, where magistrates refused to prosecute.

So away had gone the Mayflower in 1620, carrying the first dauntless seekers of freedom from an overbearing Crown and state religion. In 1649 poor Charles I's head came off and the non-conformists had their Head of State and Parliament. But it all went wrong and there, in 1660, was another King. And only a hundred years later (historically an eye-blink) a strong Quaker settlement was firmly established in Millbrook.

We have heard more than enough lately about religious dreams and urges – what do they come down to in the end? One might say, "plus ça change...." As it was Gloucestershire went on to become a stronghold of Methodism, its rural labourers, disaffected with the class system inherent in the Anglican church, were rich recruiting ground. The county boasts many old Methodist chapels. Some have become tasteful residences, but others continue as places of worship. So what is it about the countryside that attracts

---

* *A Gambling Man: Charles II and the Restoration* by Jenny Uglow.

free thinkers? Stretching green fields, empty skies, fresh air? I am not sure. But now that the Big Thaw has happened I can get off the sofa and go for a walk and look at our wide and open skies and wonder if they might not have something to do with it. And in Millbrook too.

IX

Mr Brown Goes to Washington

19 January 2010

It's not hard to think what to write about this week. Two American citizens live in this house, two US tax-payers, one from birth and one from choice, two people astounded by last week's Massachusetts election result. What happened in what you would have thought was the safest Democratic state in the Union?

Well there was a pretty feeble campaign by Ms Coakley – complete with her posters spelling Massachusetts wrong. And of course Mr – or as we must say now – Senator Brown is a dishy looking fellow, with a well-known and feisty wife, two pretty daughters and a pick-up truck. So far so Mr Smith. The Senator supports abortion rights and, in his home state, universal healthcare. He has however voted against gay marriage. A black mark for some, a legitimate view for others. He also appears to shun the real down-home folksy way with words and winks which is Mrs Palin's trademark. So things could be worse – much worse!

But what does his election mean? One paper here writes, in British election vocabulary, "In a by-election in a safe seat in a deep recession, the voters threw out the de facto incumbent". In other words they shook a warning finger at the establishment. How will the President respond to this in

his State of the Union address? How much of the vote for
Scott Brown was a vote against Obama's health care ambi-
tions, how much was the electorate getting its own back for
unemployment and credit crunch in the only way available?
Nobody really knows. It depends which poll you read,
which radio station you tune into, which newspaper you
follow. They all have different opinions. One thing is
certain, the President will have his work cut out. So will this
be his eureka moment?

His time in office to date has been distinguished by his
sense of balance, of nuance, by an awareness of the need to
bring disparate views to a workable point. Will these qual-
ities now have to go to the wall? His involvement with the
law-making powers of Congress is not dissimilar to that of
Charles II and his Parliament to which I referred last week.
Charles II was a wily fellow and in the end he got his way.
Let us hope that the President can do the same.

As must be obvious by now this is a household not just of
American voters, but Democrats at that. So of course we
care. But what's interesting is that we are not the only ones
round here who wonder what will happen, who ask
ourselves what Mr Scott Brown's arrival might portend.
Dyed-in-the-wool British neighbours chew it over, it's a
talking point at many levels. For some it just goes to show
that no politician can fix the mess we're in, for others it's a
demonstration that even in this day and age the electorate
still has the power to surprise and alarm the establishment.

Perhaps most interesting of all is that here in this small
village, where most inhabitants are middle-of–the-road, let's
get our life sorted out sort of people, the question of what
happens in America at this level is still seen as important.
We read of the vast monetary power of China, India and the
ever-growing South Americas. But we like to think that the

USA gets some things right. On the whole we are not that keen on Senator Brown. But we like the fact that there is a process which can put him where he is whether we like him or not. We also like the fact (in this house) that there are another ten months before any more Mr Browns have the chance to come our way.

Go for it Mr President.

X

To Bite the Hand that Feeds

23 February 2010

"I read much of the night and go south in the winter", wrote T. S. Eliot. Why ignore advice from such a source? So 7 February saw us heading south, with some good books. There was yet more snow on the ground, but our hearts were light. We were off to be WARM!

Our choice of destination was limited. My husband has lately been too ill to think of going anywhere; this journey, his first for eighteen months, had to be a short one. Research revealed that the Canary Islands were only four hours away and, owing to a little blip in the meridian, there was no time difference between them and the UK. So touchdown was to be Tenerife South.

We were apprehensive. Well-known haunt of plumbers, builders and expatriates on a pension, the Canaries have been called Essex-on-Sea, with Estuary English the lingua franca. But I had found a couple of places on the web which looked pretty understated, the first on Tenerife and the second, a short ferry-hop away, on La Gomera. And we were travelling with friends, so were assured of congenial company. What was to lose if we gave it a whirl?

The coast round Tenerife is for the most part a long sprawl of buildings. Apartments, hotels, theme-parks crawl up the hillsides, looking like huge insect colonies. There is nothing to recommend these views. But you can still find untouched hills, extraordinary plant zones and El Tiede – at 3718m the highest point in Spain – a living volcano, its snow-covered peak rising majestically above the cloud-line. The North-West corner of the island is relatively untouched too. We stayed there in one of the most delightful hotels I have ever encountered, a tiny pool of pleasure. An old Canarian house converted with great taste. Entertaining modern art, 30s furniture and good food. And small.

This was not to be our good fortune when we headed off to La Gomera. We particularly wanted to go there because it was Columbus's launch-pad for his epic voyages. My husband is currently helping to build a library celebrating the history of the United States, so it was a "must-see" on the Weissman itinerary. We did indeed walk through the little house where Columbus stayed and where, in the court-yard, is a well, proudly labelled (in Spanish), "This water baptized America". Most touching were the models of the ships in which Columbus sailed. Tiny, tiny, tiny – whatever else has changed in the Canaries the sea has not. Huge waves and great spouts of spray constantly reminded one of the ferocity of the ocean and the lunatic bravery which sent those early explorers on their way.

The islands need the tourists' bucks Big Time. In the 1970s a collapse in the agricultural economy sent many inhabitants off to seek work in South America. Now they can go home. Thanks to designation as a World Heritage site (1986) certain parts of La Gomera remain inviolable. As also with the Parque Nacional del Teide on Tenerife (1954). But tourism brings another death in its train. Eventually our hotel on La Gomera was a vast "resort" complex. (Reservations on the internet can go badly wrong – traditional parador goodbye!) It was perfectly possible to stay there and not leave until it was time to go home. Swimming pools, tennis lessons, water aerobics, a vast dining-hall with buffet feasts designed to please the international palate, rooms with balconies overlooking the sea or manicured gardens – the perfect place to recoup in the middle of a nasty winter. What need to find out about the island, its customs, its cuisine, its extraordinary geological history? Such venues exist throughout the archipelago.

While we were there the crisis of the euro and the Greek economy broke. It was obvious that funding from the EEC had helped put the Canaries back on their feet. Fine roads, serious town improvements, vital sustaining contributions. But what does it all mean? Paul Krugman* argues that the EEC got a bit above itself when it invented the euro – too much too soon. He compares it with the slowly evolved fiscal structure of the USA. But perhaps Europe is different? How do you work a common currency in an area which has, over thousands of years, developed very different and very specific cultures? I don't know. I am not an economist. But I do know that were I to be a Canary Islander I might occasionally wish to bite the tourist hand that feeds me. Right off. At the wrist.

*Paul Krugman is a columnist for *The New York Times* and Professor of Economics and International Affairs at Princeton. He was awarded the 2008 Nobel Prize in Economics.

XI

Just a Village Day

2 March 2010

What to write for *The Millbrook Independent* readers isn't obvious – despite similarities there are huge differences between this little village and the wider reach of a township in the great spread of America's East Coast. I'm not always sure what might provoke recognition or interest.

So I thought this week I'd just describe yesterday, Sunday. In the morning we woke to more weather gloom. Unlike you we no longer have snow, but it is unusually cold. In March last year we set the central heating to Twice, first for chilly morning hours and second to make evenings snug. Not this year. First thing it was down to the cellar to the button that makes the boiler roar away all day. Then, looking out of the window, there was our bottom paddock, completely flooded. Devoted as I am to moorhens and swans I would rather see grass and bulbs coming through down there by now. And half the new arbour lay on the ground, knocked flat by the wind. On with the boots and out in the chill to free the roses tangled in its fallen struts. That was my start.

Then lunch and a nervous recounting from my American husband of his progress with his Driving Test Theory preparation. Believe it or not, at the age of seventy plus, he must pass the British Driving Test to become an insurable driver here. (A little argument with a bus has just brought this to our notice!) There are one thousand possible questions, based on The Highway Code, plus the Hazard Perception Test. For this the computer shows fourteen simulated situations – fifteen hazards must be spotted and clicked on. Once the theory test is passed the applicant can take the practical. I have been driving for years, but I am sure I would fail the Test now!

Next came a visit to a neighbour with advanced motor neurone disease. A couple of weeks ago I went to call, taking something I thought he might enjoy reading. To my great embarrassment he told me he could no longer turn a page. Not to be able to read has to be torture, so I had offered to read to him and he had asked for some American poetry. This was our first session and Elizabeth Bishop was tucked under my arm. "The art of losing is not hard to master" seemed appropriate. As it was he spent an hour and a half giving me a lively tutorial in philosophy and I left with a demanding book list. His wife paints professionally, so I got a preview of works for an upcoming show. Another feature was meeting their new live-in carer – a large and cheerful Ghanaian lady, whose penchant for chocolate is proving testing. I thought I had problems, but catastrophic ill-health, professional demands and a not wholly sympathetic extra resident made them insignificant.

Home to struggle with dinner. We had asked a couple from the other end of the village for "kitchen supper", i.e. something cosy and simple. So I thought, lasagne. I had never made it before and I shall never make it again! Cosy yes, but simple ... there were more pots and pans than I would have needed for a feast. But it got done just in time as our friends arrived. She has had breast cancer, but it seems that the chemotherapy has succeeded. Sporting a chic pink cap while her hair returns and in thigh-high, high-heeled black boots Fliss looked fantastic and the colour has returned to her husband's cheeks. They are going to buy a flat in London for get-away moments – theatre, restaurants, opera. But they are also moving into livestock – a pig or two. They are younger than us – their son, who sells me half a dozen eggs every week, is now in trouble (for sweet-smuggling!) while their elder daughter has the first unsuitable follower – but we really like them. Since moving here they have gone for country life hot and strong with fowl, guinea pigs and an extensive vegetable garden. Several glasses of claret and some excellent port, cheese and ginger biscuits kept us happy till nearly midnight. Then their Czech male au pair came to drive them home.

And that was it really. Just a note to myself to call Monday's garden helper and cancel. You can't do much with wet cold ground. But nothing keeps a snowdrop down. So I knew the first thing I would see next day would be the long river of white snaking through my upper garden, thousands of little demonstrators firmly announcing SPRING. Death, recovery, growth, three different nationalities, painting, poetry, philosophy – in 24 hours in under a mile – who needs opera?

XII

The Beastly, the Beautiful, the Busy and the Benign

9 March 2010

It is still perishing. But the sun is out. So every window on the west side of the house has its occupation force – *viz*: huge foreign ladybirds and flies. They creep about the window-panes, basking in warmth, sure that summer is here. They drive me crazy! But there is no way to keep them out – this is an old house with cracks in the floorboards and large ancient uninsulated roof cavities. As winter approaches it is easy for the winged invaders to make their way into a nice centrally heated hibernation zone. Just occasionally we might find the odd dead body on the stairs, but essentially they are tucked away cosily, waiting for the first sunbeams. The butterflies are quite another story – they fly about inside, nestle in the curtains, perch on the houseplants. But they do not make it through till Spring. Flirtatiously beautiful they expend their last energies brightening our cold dark months, but theirs is definitely a kamikaze urge.

There has to be a moral here. No doubt the Victorians, those pillars of rectitude and certainty, would have seen the butterflies as embodiments of foolishness and waste – how much wiser to be the prudent ladybird or fly. But in today's world of use it or lose it, here today and gone tomorrow mode, maybe the butterflies are more in tune with the zeitgeist? To be cautious, frugal and wise is no bad thing, especially in the present economic disaster-zone, but we also need to be gay, light of heart and occasionally even improvident. There is, after all, no second act.

In fact for the butterflies there is an afterlife. At least for those I find here, perched, wings still spread, dry and dead. Unlike the beastly flies and lady-birds which I vacuum up with zeal, the exquisite corpses – Red Admirals and Peacock Blues mostly – are carefully wrapped and put in a box and sent to London. That's where my five year old grandson lives and at his thoroughly urban school they have a nature table. Mostly autumn leaves, worms and, soon, tadpoles. Not many butterflies. Until Freddie takes in his Gloucestershire consignment. They make a rather good teaching tool on natural diversity and, since global warming is now a subject discussed at all levels, a perfect example of what could be lost if we are not careful. All the children's parents recycle, it's a regular feature in every London borough, but how to make that interesting to a child? The coloured wings of my corpses are educative magic.

Because this is an old house with lathe and plaster walls we have another winged species in residence. Last summer we could hear a persistent low roaring sound – I thought some garden machine had been left with its engine running. But no. It was a swarm of bees – a great black spiralling cloud. After about twenty minutes of hanging around at our north-east corner they found a gap in the stone roof-tiles and in they went, to remain there for the rest of the season. What we don't yet know is whether or not the queen and her workers will have survived this bitter and lengthy cold.

And it is still too soon to know, even though we do go and look up to see whether any lone scout is out yet.

If the colony has survived we shall be hosts to a perfect compromise. Wise and frugal but also beautiful, the bees will not feature on the nature table, but will rather buzz about being busy and benign. I guess we can get some pictures when Freddie comes to visit and he will just have to take those to school instead!

XIII

Mothering Sunday

16 March 2010

Today has been delightful. My daughter and her son were here with us so two generations celebrated Mothering Sunday together. Courtesy of Rebecca my bouquet was delivered by Interflora, while her flowers were picked in the garden by Freddie. My fine flourish of daffodils and jonquils was complemented by his snowdrops, scillas and anemones in a little twist of silver foil, so they would survive their journey home to London. Lunch was in the dining room with the fire blazing – not usual when it's just us guys hanging out – "But," said five year old Fred, "it's a special day." Similarly happy scenes were being played out countrywide.

Mothering Sunday here harks back to the days when Christianity was the ruling ethic. It is always the fourth Sunday in Lent, so, unlike the US, where Mother's Day is fixed as 9 May, the UK date, along with Easter, changes every year. It was once the custom for children to be given this Lenten Sunday off, so as to visit their mothers, since, way back then, it was quite usual for children over the age of ten to be in work. Boys were apprenticed to a trade and girls to domestic service. Tradition has it that on their walk home on this special day the children would pick flowers for Mum from the Spring hedgerows, so a loving bouquet remains at the heart of this now almost wholly secularised festival.

I checked out Mother's Day on the web. Nowadays it is celebrated worldwide – in Bolivia, since 1927, it is 27 May, in Bangladesh it is the second Sunday in May, in India it is 19 August, and in China, since 1997, it is also the second Sunday in May, to name but a few. So how has this Christian custom spread so widely? For a start it turns out that it was not originally a Christian idea. Like many other major festivals of the church – think Saturnalia – its roots are far older. The ancient Greeks celebrated the festival of Cybele around the Vernal Equinox (15-18 March) and the Romans had Matronalia, dedicated to Juno, even then a day when Mums got gifts.

The last century saw the creation of International Women's Day and, as an offshoot of that concept, many more countries took their cue to establish and celebrate a Mother's Day, even though dates vary. In Japan it is linked to the birthday of the Empress Kojun (mother of the Emperor Akihito) and in most Arab countries 21 March – the first day of Spring – is the day. Overall it is a charming, if somewhat sentimental, marker of women's unique role, although it does not carry the weight originally intended. It was to show that "Women had a responsibility to shape their societies at a political level". But you've got to start somewhere.

There is one sad tale. In America Anna Jarvis of Grafton, West Virginia was determined that mothers should be celebrated and as a result of her continued petitioning, along with the efforts of Julia Ward Howe, President Woodrow Wilson, in 1914, declared 9 May as Mother's Day. However Anna Jarvis became so incensed by the commercialisation of the holiday that eventually she opposed it as vigorously as she had campaigned for its introduction. In the end she was declared insane and put into an asylum. Her bills there were, until her death, paid by a flower industry group, the Floral Exchange. I wonder why!

Right now both the Prime Minister and the Leader of the Opposition are wheeling out their wives – Sarah Brown and Samantha Cameron – to provide a little colour for the imminent election campaign. "… the hand that rocks the cradle/ Is the hand that rules the world", wrote William Ross Wallace in 1865. I wonder whether Mr Brown and Mr Cameron remember the lines – they seem to be keen to demonstrate the role of wife and mother power. Anna Jarvis would have approved!

XIV

Death and Taxes

23 March 2010

"Nothing is certain but death and taxes", said Benjamin Franklin. Here where Spring, seemingly at last arrived with sunshine and flowers, has now done a vanishing act and left grey skies and teeming rain, the certainty of taxes is on everybody's mind. The fiscal year ends on 5 April so the demands of the Inland Revenue and of the boroughs and county councils are dropping on all doorsteps. Probably the only really happy people in England right now are accountants.

Income tax is set by the government, but Council Tax – our equivalent of US property tax – varies from region to region. In a major city such as London each borough sets its own rate, but here we are subject to the Cotswold District Council, itself part of Gloucestershire County Council. The tax levied from local residents is supplemented by central government, at a rate that varies from year to year. Essentially it is meant to fund education, policing, firefighting, extensive social services, environmental efforts such as recycling, waste collection and road repairs – 3,300 miles in Gloucestershire. To the forefront here at the moment is flood work – since 2007s disastrous floods £11 million has been invested in flood risk management within the county – £1.4 million of that on cleaning highway drains.

Council Tax replaced what used to be called rates and also put paid to the ill-advised notion of the so-called Poll Tax (an idea which, after major rioting on the streets of London, finally brought down Margaret Thatcher). Properties were valued and banded – the lowest being Band A and the highest Band H. So far so equitable, but in fact there is one major flaw. A property in Band H can be a substantial house such as ours, or a castle with a hundred rooms or more. On a house worth just over £2 million the Council Tax is the same as that on a house worth £22 million. So the rich are getting off lightly. My husband argues that this has two root causes. Not only British law, essentially established by the landed classes, for a long time the only people to sit in the House of Commons, but also the British attitude to wealth, combine to protect the propertied classes. Whereas in America industry, trade and the stock market were the source and measure of wealth, in this country land and property played those roles. There is therefore, he says, an inherited imbalance in any government's approach to property. The counter-argument is that the better-off may get a good deal on their Council Tax, but they pay far higher income tax, which tax is recycled into national subsidies for local areas. But you might justly say that the notion of there being a point at which tax on the home can go no higher is pretty silly.

Interestingly enough it has never been an issue on which people spend much thought. Partly this is due to the belief that if you draw attention to a tax it is likely to go up and partly because it is an intrinsically dull topic. Our Parish Newsletter for February had two solid pages on Cotswold District Council's Key Budget Proposals for 2010/2011, written by our local Councillor. These ranged from Council Utility Bills to Travel Tokens, to Car Parking and Leisure

Charges, to Local Development Framework (LDF) to name
but a few. The paragraph on LDF was a marvel of jargon –
"robust as possible", "watertight policy", "a must-do".
The brain reels and the voter tunes out.

   Yet these things affect us daily. Perhaps that's why we let
them slide through on the nod, while getting exercised on
the rights or wrongs of a war, or the EEC, or industrial
action. You can't really get too worked up over Parking
Charges. Were Ben Franklin to be writing now he might
have added a word: – nothing is certain but death, taxes –
and drains.

XV

Now It Can Be Told

30 March 2010

There's something I've wanted to write about for some time, but it didn't seem appropriate. You can't meddle in a debate that's not your own. But ever since President Obama's Health Care triumph on Sunday, 21 March, I've been looking forward to knocking this piece out for *The Millbrook Independent*.

Let me tell you a story. In November, 2008 a man of sixtynine couldn't feel his backside, his thighs and the bottoms of his feet. They were just numb. So he waited a while and they got even number. An immediate appointment with the local doctor, who sent him at once to his nearest major hospital, the Great Western, was followed by an MRI scan. This revealed a condition known as Cauda Equina – a ruptured disc that had entered his spinal cord. At 10:30 pm a surgeon came up from theatre and got on the phone to a specialist at another hospital. The man was kept overnight in the Great Western, but the following morning, after a consultation meeting by the resident surgical team, he was transferred 50 miles by ambulance to the John Radcliffe in Oxford, one of the foremost teaching hospitals in the UK, where it was felt the expertise available was greater. A surgeon came to talk to him at once. He explained how

serious the condition was and what a very difficult operation   was   needed.   But   without   treatment   double
incontinence, paralysis from the waist down and even death
could result. The patient signed the consent form – what
was to lose? Then the surgeon went to scrub up and the man
was prepped and sent down to the operating room. Four
hours later the surgeon returned and, beaming from ear to
ear, said to the man's wife, "I think I've done it." The
patient was then kept on the intensive care ward for a week,
after which he was allowed to go home. Subsequent follow-
up appointments were made with both the surgeon and his
next-in-command. His life was saved.

This treatment, totalling, at a conservative estimate,
£75,000 in all, did not cost the patient one penny. Nor was
any other patient in the J. R. neurosurgical unit paying a
bean. They were a complete cross-section of society, of
varying creed, class and colour, united only by being very
sick indeed and by being tended by the best. That is the
point of the National Health Service.

It has its downside. Hospitals are often antiquated buildings, nursing staff sometimes have less than perfect English,
if your condition is not life-threatening you may have to
wait for a slot. But you will be treated. No one in this
country is ever in the position of not being able to afford
medical care. If you want to have Private Treatment you
may and many people choose to have medical insurance.
This enables them to skip a queue and to spend their hospital time in fancier venues. But as the specialists and
consultants work in the public and private sectors, their
expertise and skill is available in both.

It is not just hospitalization that is free. A visit to the GP,
follow-up consultations, radio and/or chemotherapy, MRIs,
brain scans – all are there for everybody. It is probably the

UK's finest achievement and a permanent memorial to the post-war Labour government of 1948. It is efficient, comprehensive and egalitarian.

To us this side of the water this reform adds real lustre to the United States and shows yet again that when America wants to do something it can. Even when it is something really difficult. And just in case you think my story of the man whose life was saved at no charge is an exaggeration, I'll tell you now, the man was my husband.

XVI

Easter Day

6 April 2010

This is a country with a state religion. We are all very relaxed about it. Nobody is obliged to be an Anglican and indeed many UK citizens are not. But when it comes to Easter Day you do notice that the newspapers feature religious items.

Not necessarily however those concerning doctrine. To get us started, on Good Friday *The Times* had a wonderful photograph of the Queen leaving Derby Cathedral having attended the Maundy Thursday service there on its 800th anniversary. She is eighty-three and looked as cheerful as a jay bird. It appears that she dropped her Service Paper and the little girl chosen to present her with a posy had picked it up for her. It's quite tricky when Her Majesty does something not in the schedule, but clearly this small child had just thought, "I must help this old lady," and with no regard for protocol just did what she'd do for her own granny. The Queen looked delighted and beaming. So that was a good start.

Next day we had the Archbishop of Canterbury, a wise old bird, long on the beard but short on charisma, going for the Roman church's current difficulties with a quiet undercut, "It is not just a problem for the Church, it is a problem for everybody in Ireland." And *Private Eye*, a satirical magazine that's been going now for about fifty years and is famous for its front covers, had a picture of the Pope giving his Easter address from the balcony with a speech balloon from a couple in the crowd saying, "It used to be that young boys wanted to enter the priesthood....". The mini dust-up continued when clergy condemned Canterbury for being "thoughtless and unhelpful" and finally the Archbishop of Dublin responded to our Archbishop's apologetic phone call by saying that there had been "some unfortunate words".

Such things happen all the time – as with the UN, NATO, UNESCO et al so it is with the differing churches of the Christian faith – but this latest spat became headline news because it was Easter Day. The Press would normally have attended neither the Archbishop's sermon nor the Pontiff's address. But just like the smoke from the Vatican chimney or pre-election Gallup Polls there are moments when religious comment is seen as having a social relevance beyond its purely doctrinal import. Such was the case this Easter Sunday.

Here in the village there were the usual Easter observances, a particularly spectacular peel of pre-service bells and an Easter egg drop from the church tower when the Sunday morning service was over. A good and cheerful, if chilly, time was had by all. And that is the comfort of a religious observance embedded in the rituals of the state. No doubt many people, believers and non-believers alike, read the media's details of the rift and rumpus with interest. But when it came to the crunch those who wanted to go to church and celebrate a particularly sacred moment in the Christian calendar trundled off anyway. Because in a small place that's what you do, no matter what the guys at the top

are saying. It is as much a part of English country life as
riding to hounds or the summer fête. In uncertain times –
and who could deny that these are such – some things just
potter on as usual.

My newspaper, *The Guardian*, a fine old organ of non-
conformist and left-wing comment, had an interesting
column today, discussing the recent emergence of numerous
books on religion, both pro and ante. It is interesting how
New Atheism, most spectacularly embodied by Richard
Dawkins, has sparked a resurgence of books in defence of
God. As the article ended, "God hasn't attracted this inten-
sity of debate for decades". This is I think true. But if I
didn't live in a country with a state religion I doubt whether
such an article would have appeared on Easter Monday.

But so what. It is Easter and both Good Friday and Easter
Monday are Bank Holidays. So believer or not, Anglican or
other, people have had two lovely days off.

This has to be both joyful and cheering, as the daffodils
crowd the roadside verges.

XVII

They're Off!

13 April 2010

Lately that's been the key-note cry. Saturday, 10 April was Grand National day, a race watched by millions of Brits and right now, another horse-race is underway. I refer of course to our up-coming General Election. On 6 April the Prime Minister went to Buckingham Palace to ask the Queen to dissolve Parliament and on the twelfth it was duly dissolved. This means polling day is 6 May. The bookmakers are busy!

The Cotswolds are horse country, with hunting, racing at Cheltenham and point-to-points countywide, while small boys, large girls, estate agents, plumbers and the gentry perched on noble steeds abound on both highways and byways. So the National (as it is fondly called) was a particularly top event round here. There were queues at the betting-shops as even those who would not venture five pence on a game of marbles waited to place their wagers. It was a big field, forty horses, no starting-gates, just riders jockeying around to find a spot they liked the look of. Only one false start this year – and a horse that decided he didn't want to run – and they were off. Injury meant that the favourite, Big Fella Thanks, had a last minute substitute jockey, so his odds fell and in the end Don't Push It came through to take the race at 10-1. He had not been considered a contender, but in a last minute flurry the odds changed. Those who had put their money on early in the day, when odds were still long, did very nicely. It's the race that gets everybody going. The supermarket was half-empty when I nipped in at lunch time – on a Saturday? – and there wasn't much road traffic. Pre-race barbecues or pre-race drinks at the pub kept everyone busy. Nationwide it is a totally cheerful and slightly irresponsible day.

The other race does not generate the same enthusiasm. Of course bookmakers give odds and of course bets are laid. But this year especially the nation is not gripped with excitement by its chance to change the government. In part this is the result of the world financial crisis but it is also attributable to a general disaffection with MPs after the scandal of Parliamentary expenses. People don't really believe that government, of whatever colour, will change their lives and, perhaps more importantly, they feel no connection with those fighting for power. It's easy with a horse – it looks good, you like its name, the jockey's wife once danced with a man who knows a man you know. But the people who want you to give them the reins in the parliamentary race are frequently far removed from your frame of reference. All candidates will be galloping round their constituency, kissing babies and visiting the sick, just to show that they are good guys at heart. And indeed some of them are. But those at the top, the controllers – who knows them? There will be contrasting manifestos of what each party will do once they are in government – you can put your bet on the one that appeals the most. Or, as is often the case, you can make your mark just to demonstrate that you have had enough of the present lot, whatever the other guys are offering. You can also simply spoil your ballot to show you think they are all hopeless.

Round here pretty well every man and his dog votes Conservative. Large fields of freshly-sown crops are already sporting billboards in support of the Tories. Occasionally you will see a UKIP banner too (UK Independence Party, with its two-word manifesto, Goodbye Europe). Our MP has been in place for many years and does not feel the wind of chance around his ankles. For him it's a done deal. But for the voting population as a whole it's a three-horse race. The Liberal Democrats – outsiders – New Labour, the Prime Minister's party and the Tories, trying to re-invent themselves as the party who care, odds about even. At this point I wouldn't like to bet on either of the main contenders, but, more to the point, neither would the voters. With the National what you see or what you fancy is where you put your money. And it's over pretty fast. But the ongoing contest with its far-reaching implications doesn't give the same buzz. It goes on too long – and who knows what the future holds whoever wins? Maybe we should just put the leaders of the parties on well-matched mounts, shout, "They're off!" and see who comes in first.

XVIII

Silence

20 April 2010

Your Editor mentioned to me that this was to be the Green
issue of *The Millbrook Independent,* with reports on
organic farming, raw milk and similar topics as a celebration of Earth Day. So I did some local research and was
ready to go with the flow. But then something SO extraordinary happened that no other topic would do. I refer of
course to the eruption of Eyjafjallajokull.

It is almost impossible to believe that an eruption in
Iceland could not only stop air traffic all over Northern
Europe but also make the Atlantic Ocean a no-fly zone. Yet
that is what has happened. No planes have taken off from
British airports since 15 April. The skies are empty. And it
is wonderful. There is no overarching noise.

On Saturday we had to be in London and, after shopping,
we picnicked in Cavendish Square, along with many others
making the most of the year's first gloriously warm day.
Normally the air would be threaded through with the
vapour trails from jets heading for or leaving from
Heathrow, making the sky look like so much unravelling
yarn. But there was nothing. For people my age it was a
return to childhood, when you could lie on your back, gaze
up into the brilliant blue above and see only emptiness. But

for the young it was a completely new experience. Something ever-present had just been Turned Off. Later that day we went to my daughter's birthday party. None of her friends, aged between say 35 – 40, had ever seen a London sky with nothing in it. They loved it. And most of all they loved the silence. And later on, after dark, there were just stars.

Of course for a lot of people this has been a truly disastrous occurrence. Pupils on family half-term breaks can't get back to the first day of school. But that is probably a good thing, since a great many teaching staff are also stranded! Many travellers have insurance that does not cover the extra costs of staying on. Business packages can't be transported between the US and Europe. The economy is losing money big-time. Whitney Houston had to take a ferry boat to Ireland and John Cleese took a taxi from Norway to Belgium – the fare, £3,300. Several dignitaries, including President Obama, could not get to the state funeral of the late President of Poland. Airlines, already in trouble in the post-downturn, are losing millions of pounds. The Prime Minister is making plans to send naval vessels to rescue some of the 200,000 Brits stuck abroad. It is chaotic.

But eventually it will end. The volcano will calm down, the air will clear, normal service will be resumed. Summer plans will be made and foreign holidays booked. Some may choose to go by boat, just to be on the safe side, most will take a chance because they only have two weeks' break. And those evaporating vapour trails will once again be threading the skies.

Shall we have learnt anything? Probably not. Man's ability to transport himself and his goods far and wide won't be lost. We shall still buy flowers from Chile, green beans from Kenya, pineapple chunks from Ghana – such exports support national economies and cannot be allowed to fail. But looking at a list of events that could be affected if this crisis continues I am struck by their international nature. US stars may not make a London film premiere, US publishers may not make the London Book Fair, elite athletes may not make the coming London Marathon, cricket and football fixtures could be affected. In one way it is dotty, but in another the list shows just how thoroughly our lives are interwoven now, planet-wide.

So maybe the volcano has done us all a favour. It has reminded us of the terrifying powers the earth holds – the tsunami, the recent earthquakes in Chile and Tibet – shocks quite beyond our power to control or predict. But the list of events that could be affected shows something else. How our societies are now so involved, how much we are all inter-linked. How closely therefore must we all work to solve the problems our advanced civilization has created. There could not be a more effective Earth Day poster. But when it all gets back to normal, I shall miss the silence.

XIX

The Yellow Peril

27 April 2010

When I was young the phrase "the yellow peril" meant only one thing. The Chinese. They were out there in their millions and they were going to destroy us. Such was a child's legacy of Empire. I don't know whether it was the being yellow that did it – Africa held many black people and India was entirely populated by people who were brown – but in some strange way it was only the yellow people who were seen as having the power to do us in. Perhaps a legacy of Dr Fu Manchu?

Memory of TYP stirred this week. Spring is finally in full flood and our lawns and paddock are *covered* in dandelions. This fiendish plant is not only native to North America, but also to China, from whence it came to Britain to make every gardener's life a nightmare. The Yellow Peril indeed. Forget the Opium Wars, Communism, or the flood of consumer goods at prices vastly below our own, the dandelion is the true instrument of revenge.

But then I looked it up. *Taraxacum officinale.* There are twenty-three related species, including the rubber-producing Russian dandelion and the white dandelion from Japan. And as well as the things all children know, such as how to tell the time with them, or how to make them into beautiful necklaces, these wretched weeds have a long and august history. The Romans learnt their properties from the Celts, they were planted in monastic herb gardens. They are edible and nutritious. They contain anti-cancer properties, may be used as a diuretic – perhaps that is why the French call them *pissenlits* – and are high in potassium and vitamin C. They can serve as a detox agent. On the natural world front they are loved by both bees and butterflies.

There are three very special cultivars – including one with the musical name *Améliore à Coeur Plein* – and dandelion leaves, with their a slightly bitter taste, closely akin to endive, can be used in salads. As I read on I began to wonder whether the dandelion had helped us win the war – nettle soup and similar home-grown hedgerow horrors were a staple of the British war and post-war diet. Not a regimen I would particularly wish to re-visit. But Japan, Greece, France and the UK have traditional dandelion recipes and Red Dandelion Greens Salad features on another current related website. The dandelion may be blanched or sautéed and, in winter, eaten raw and unadorned, as by then it will have lost its very bitter tang. Red Dandelion Greens salad requires sautéing with olive oil and garlic and just a dash of pecorino fresco. Other recipes suggest adding onion, chilli pepper or white wine.

So suddenly my lawn is not a gardener's nightmare covered in a horrible yellow rash. It is a food source. It is a way for me to do my bit towards saving the planet. I should rejoice. But I do not. They look ghastly. "A weed," so the saying goes, "is a plant in the wrong place". These words describe my dandelion flotilla precisely. So tomorrow when the gardener comes there will be quite a bit of digging up and dragging out of taproots. But knowledge is power, so we will set aside one corner and allow some to flourish. We grow carrots and broad beans and beetroots and such, so why not have a go with another sort of vegetable? At least I shall know that the frequently mentioned very necessary caution, be sure the dandelion you are about to consume has not been sprayed with weed-killer, does not apply. Our dandelion bed will be a protected zone.

However there is one plant/weed that is a bridge too far. I found a recipe for Apple and Knotweed Pie. This vile plant will bring down walls and ruin paths – when I see it I slay it. I take an eye-dropper and drip weedkiller into its hollow stem. The recipe says knotweed tastes like rhubarb. Well we grow rhubarb and, to paraphrase James Thurber, I say it's knotweed and the hell with it.

XX

Horses Galore

4 May 2010

This weekend the world's most famous three-day event took place, thirty-five miles from here. I refer of course to Badminton. It pulls in the biggest crowd of any UK sporting occasion – on cross-country day approximately 130,000 people turn out.

This year the weather was vile, cold and rainy, but it didn't stop spectators from gathering at the Duke of Beaufort's country pile to see what feats of horsemanship might be achieved. Even someone not the outright winner could make a real showing in the dressage, cross-country or jumping. And for the British spectator there was the added interest of seeing who might be our hopefuls for the 2012 Olympics.

The Olympics are somewhat of a sore spot here. In 1948 the British team did very badly indeed and it was this that prompted the 10th Duke to inaugurate Badminton in 1949. National pride would be greatly boosted if we could do better this time, with the Games back on our turf. Since eventing became an Olympic sport in 1912 the British have done very well indeed. Champions have emerged – The Princess Royal, her first husband, Capt. Mark Phillips and their daughter Zara – to name but a few. But not at home – yet!

XXI

Little and Large

11 May 2010

As no doubt *The Millbrook Independent* readers know the UK has just held a General Election. I think I might have mentioned it a couple of times! Well, we have indeed had an election, but so far we don't have a government. The idiosyncrasies of our system mean that no one party has enough votes to take control. It is quite different from the US – we don't, despite the best efforts of the media – have a presidential system. We don't vote for the leader we favour, we vote for the party whose policies we approve. And this we do by voting for the person we wish to see represent our constituency in the House of Commons. With a Parliamentary majority one party or another is in power. This time there is no majority and so the horse-trading in Westminster is at fever-pitch. Both the Labour and the Conservative parties want Mr Clegg to join their dance and he is playing it close to his chest right now. Will he go for giving our present Prime Minister a biff on the nose by supporting the Conservatives? Or will he shack up with the party – i.e. Labour – which promises Electoral Reform and Proportional Representation? The nation waits.

I am as gripped as anyone. However tomorrow we are at last off to call in my 70th birthday present to my husband.

So it's up early, a long drive and three nights in what looks like a comfortable hotel. It sounds quite simple. But it is not. A note for the gardener is needed, with keys attached, as is also one for the postman and an arrangement for the newspapers. Not to mention the watering of the plants. Military planning has nothing on organizing leaving your house for a few days.

And then of course there is the question of what to wear, counting out socks, shirts and underwear and the ever-present English dilemma of what about the weather? Fur coat, raincoat, heavy boots, sensible shoes or none of the above? Also, as this jaunt is meant to be a bit of fun, what to whack in the suitcase to change into for dinner to look flirty and light-hearted in the candlelight?

The terrible truth is that I am as much preoccupied with these trivialities as I am with the state of the nation. True, the latter hangs over me in a dark cloud of unknowing. But nevertheless I do know what we shall be doing for the next four days and have to get us organized. Focus on the immediate is required. Perhaps, writ large, that is what prevents everyone from going up in a cloud of smoke. Man proposes, God disposes, but you still have to feed the cat.

There is, for me, one other element to our outing. As my husband happily pokes about in the Ducal library I am going to visit the place of my birth – Willersley Castle, a two hundred year old building erected by Sir Richard Arkwright, inventor of the Spinning Jenny. Sir Richard's machine enabled this country to be the supreme supplier of cotton goods in the nineteenth century. Well, that's all changed, as indeed has the status of his grand home. It is now a Temperance Hotel with strong Christian influence. I don't think I will linger long! But after sixty plus years it will be fun to check out where I first drew breath.

And by the time we come home perhaps the question of who's in charge here will have been settled. Governments come and governments go – as do industrialists like Richard Arkwright – while the rest of us potter on from the cradle to the grave dealing with the trivia. But the trivia is a comfort – and we can't do without it.

XXII

There's No Place Like Home

18 May 2010

Last week we headed north, to enjoy my husband's seventieth birthday present. Our destination was Chatsworth, where he was to have two days in the library. For a man who has spent forty-five years looking at antiquarian volumes heaven could not hold more.

The Cavendishes have lived at Chatsworth since the 16th century, when Bess of Hardwick and Sir William Cavendish, using his reward for services to King Henry VIII, built themselves a house. In 1694 life looked up even more. William and Mary created William Cavendish Duke, in gratitude for his helping them to the throne. This ambitious man had rebuilt Chatsworth as a Baroque palace even before his promotion and that is what stands today. For the 12th Duke it is still home.

It sits in 400 hectares of the Derbyshire Peak District. This is sheep country and the high bare hills are forbidding. Not so the park. The 4th Duke (1720-64) hired Capability Brown to create a suitable setting. He wanted 'natural' countryside and after 50,000 man and horse days of labour, the modification of the River Derwent and the tidying up of a village, this effect was achieved. Then came Georgiana, famous for her beauty, her politics and her gambling. Next was the "Bachelor" Duke, whose Head Gardener was William Paxton, inventor of the heated greenhouse and designer of the Crystal Palace. The Cavendishes have always held a high profile in English life. The present Duke's father became Duke because his brother William, (wife, Kathleen Kennedy, sister to Jack) was killed in action, He inherited the dukedom with an 80% Death Duty Tax – equivalent to about £100 million in today's money. And history became reality.

Now for nine months each year the house and grounds are open. The Stables hold restaurants and boutique environments for garden necessities, kitchen and housewares. There is a Farm Shop. There are Events. It is a multi-million pound operation. History is the product, the public is the consumer. The Duke you might say is the CEO.

It could only happen here. The wealth of the Cavendish family is beyond reckoning. Their house is stuffed with objects of unbelievable beauty. And that is in the parts on public view. The private apartments hold many greater treasures. My husband's estimate of the library's value is in hundreds of millions of pounds. Not just for the Henry Cavendish science library, the Burlington architecture collection, or the gorgeous flower and bird books, but for a four century sequence of a family's reading life. So why is nobody shouting, "Off with their heads!"?

Put simply, this palace matters, both to those who work there and those who visit. Visitors see history at close hand, staff and volunteers become part of something that, though ferociously grand, cannot manage without them. The present Duke and Duchess interact with the public, the Guide is welcoming and inclusive. And the Duke pays rent to The Chatsworth House Trust. It is wonderfully clever. The public feels privileged to support privilege.

In a similar position Earl Spencer (brother of the late Princess Diana) is to have a sale at Christies in July. He aims to raise £10 million to invest in Althorp, to leave it in a state his son "can enjoy." "The ceilings are too low" for the Guernico. Estimate £5-£8 million. Preposterous. And we, the public, love it.

Russian oligarchs hoover up treasures for their grand houses. Chinese entrepreneurs are doing the same. So what's the difference? Just history's gloss? Or the confidence to support the new? At Chatsworth modern works are in both house and garden. Patronage is a privilege of riches. You might say that Bill Gates with his ultra-modern home is continuing a great tradition.

So who are the lucky ones? Us, or those whose efforts to maintain splendour give them sleepless nights and hours of accountancy? Hard to say. But on balance I am glad I can still wallow in vicarious glory and do not long to hear the rattle of the tumbrels!

XXIII

Flower Power

25 May 2010

Last week saw one of the UK's great international events. Americans, Japanese, Germans, Scandinavians, people from India, people from Africa, all were hugger-mugger in a tent. And a good British turnout made up the numbers. I refer of course to the Chelsea Flower Show.

For five days the grounds of the Royal Hospital, Chelsea become gardening's Mecca.

Secateurs, pruning shears, gloves, wellies, sculptures, furniture, water-features, mowers – garden-themed paraphernalia of every kind is on display. Not to mention the lavish possibilities of champagne, smoked salmon, light snacks or a good solid sandwich to enable the compulsive plants-person to keep going for twelve hours viewing. A friend, in her eighties, got up at four in the morning so as to be there on the dot for the 8:00 am opening. I only managed a five-hour stint, starting at midday. Dazed and exhausted I fell into a taxi at five, clutching information packs and a crowded notebook, vowing "never again."

And that's what most people think as they leave. But back they go, year after year. On all sides nurserymen and women greet old acquaintances, reporting on the success or otherwise of the past year's plantings. So what makes terminal fatigue of no account?

It has to be the plants. The Show Gardens, designed by experts at the top of their game, are wonderful. But difficult to see through the throng, unless you are six feet tall or have sharp elbows. The Show's heart is the Great Pavilion, where over one hundred nurseries and specialists display their wares.

According to temperament this is a place of either complete gloom or exaltation. The flowers you have proudly nurtured through the year pale into nothingness beside the superb examples of their kind arrayed on all sides. Lupins glow with colour, their perfect spires martially erect, delphiniums make an equally tall and proud wall, hostas, untouched by slug or snail, spread huge voluptuous leaves. Roses are perfection, lilies the same. And as for the vegetables... they are works of art, glowing, gleaming globes of achievement. Oh dear, you lament, my carrots will NEVER look like that, nor my zucchini neither. Each plant on display has been brought to perfection. You are stunned by the parade of richness and beauty the earth can produce.

On all sides the professionals are sympathetic, they give advice, they submit with grace to the occasional harangue from a proud amateur as to how they might do things better. Cultivation leaflets are available, lists of plants suitable for tricky areas abound, a kind of collective mania for growth pulses through both exhibitors and spectators. As the afternoon wears on the huge marquee becomes ever more crowded and a passionate hum rises – the gardening swarm has settled.

It is of course an entrepreneurial event – exhibitors of both goods and plants hope to attract customers for the coming year. Many a visitor is chasing something they must have and cannot get at their local garden centre. Consumerism does not stop at the Flower Show entrance. But at Chelsea it seems rather benign. You can buy the plant, but you have to make it grow. You can buy the ornament, but you have to make the spot in the bed to place it, you have to design the view from the ultimate garden chair. So income takes second place to knowledge and taste, for once the old probably will achieve more than the young. All in all, in an economic climate of doom, Chelsea picks up the spirits. Volcanoes, tsunamis, oil spills – Nature is fierce, but sometimes oh so beautiful. And we can join in.

XXIV
Heartbreak Hills

8 June 2010

I was in Athens last week and all ready to write about the tumbling economy and the effects of teargas. But then I got home to find a subject far more relevant to readers in a country town – the terrible shootings in Cumbria. Twelve killed and eleven seriously wounded by a man on the rampage who finally turned his gun on himself.

The country is in shock. You in the US are more used to this than we – you gave us "going postal" – and your landmass is so vast that the population can to some extent distance itself from truly shocking events. Not for want of sympathy, but simply because they are often far far away.

England is so small that that effect does not take hold. The fact that a local taxi-driver could get up one morning and shoot first his twin-brother, then his solicitor and then a fellow cabbie, before moving on to murder people with whom he had no connection whatever but who just happened to be outdoors at the time has left people aghast. Especially in locales such as ours, small, rural and relatively close-knit. Even the professions of the dead ring bells here – mole-catcher, farmer, church volunteer, bird sanctuary owner – these are country people's skills. We are surrounded by lush bursting summer green. How could such violence breed in such natural beauty? This is the question being asked in the pub.

The newspapers – tabloids and broadsheets alike – have had a field day. Reporters have scanned the man's past for hints of trouble, he was a loner, he went on exotic holidays, he had debts, but nothing even hints at the loss of human feeling on such a scale. The police have come in for a pasting – why did it take them so long to catch him? My gardener has a straightforward reply to that. "The roads, all them back roads," he said, "you can't tell where anybody is. Just like round here. You can give anyone the slip if you know the back roads."

And it's true. There is a warren of back roads here – after thirteen years I still don't know the half of them. But the cab-drivers do. On Saturday our local man brought us home down a succession of roads I'd never been on – "Best way to avoid the traffic jam at the Wildlife Park," was his explanation. "I've got my escape routes all over".

And the killer had his.

In the end we cannot know the answer, because there really isn't one. Cumbria is one of the most beautiful areas of England. You can walk for miles over high bare hills where the skies seem to go on forever. Why it should have been the scene of so horrible a massacre is inexplicable. But one man's escape can become another's prison. "Humankind cannot bear very much reality," wrote T.S. Eliot. In the starkness of the hills you face yourself. Not always a pleasure and perhaps for this one man not to be borne. But, despite the questioning, in this country community we are still giving thanks for our neighbours.

XXV

Charity Begins at Home

15 June 2010

The Cotswold summer is in full swing. This means that, come rain or shine, a charitable event is taking place in pretty much every village in the district. Kempsford has just seen Safari Supper on 12 June and Open Gardens the following day. Being far too busy doing last minute weeding and tying-in, the Safari Supper passed me by, but by Open Gardens kick-off lawns and flowerbeds were ready for the viewers' gaze. The aim was to raise money for the Village Hall. I am not quite sure what Safari Supper was in aid of – I think the restoration of the church organ.

Such events provoke high feeling in a small community. The Safari Supper guys are seen as rather an exclusive group, making for the starting point in the early evening, gussied up to the nines. I just hoped none of them would notice me as in muddy trousers and rumpled shirt I tried to tack an over-exuberant Francis Lester rose back to the driveway wall. The gardening group also has its internal differences – some say "They must take me as they find me," and others, like me, obsess for perfection. There is also feeling when some of the houses with fine gardens decline to take part. Potential theft is cited as a reason, or invasion of privacy and, in one case, the presence of a pre-booked paying group.

But, come the hour, all we owners of gardens on show for a good cause feel solidarity and pride. One or two nip round to have a quick look at what others have achieved before taking up their post on their own plot. For once the event is under way you must remain in situ and in view. I just got busy with my trowel – if people wanted to talk to me they could, but if they preferred to stroll round in peace it was easy to pass by the industrious owner's behind sticking up from a border. The odd visitor will ask a question, but most just walk round observing. I was rather disappointed that nobody asked me the name of a single rose, especially as I had spent all week making sure I knew them all! But it was time I did that anyway, so the exercise wasn't wasted.

Five o'clock was close of play and it was off to the pub to meet up, compare notes and congratulate ourselves – and of course to draw the raffle. Tickets to the famed Malvern Flower Show and a sundial were among the prizes. Less grand but just as welcome was a homemade cake. This was a real village event, so a few tasty pieces of gossip emerged as the second glass of white wine went down tired and dry throats! Bonus!

In real terms the amount of money raised – £531 – was trivial. The Village Hall needs disabled access, roof repairs and numerous other improvements – the afternoon's take was a drop in the bucket. But everyone felt pleased – they had worked as a team, got to know a new face or two – and shown Kempsford's community spirit was alive and well. These are hard times and worse are on the horizon. Goodness knows what next week's Budget will bring. But for three hours we all did our bit, and, in a funny sort of way, felt we'd put down a marker for the coming bleak days.

XXVI

Something Nasty in the Woodshed

22 June 2010

Thrift is the watchword. Save the planet, save the nation's finances. We can't do much about the latter other than pay taxes, but we are certainly up to speed on the former. Never let it be said that we in the Cotswolds are behind the times. Recycling is de rigueur and the District Council endlessly inventive on waste collection procedures. To date they have supplied us with black wheelie bins, green wheelie bins, small green compost bins and fine plastic sacks emblazoned with the Council's logo. Not to mention the stylish bright blue, heavy-duty, plastic carry-alls for our cardboard. It is quite taxing to stay abreast of these containers and I have been reprimanded for putting an envelope with a paper front and a cardboard back into cardboard-waste in its entirety. I received notice of a substantial fine should this misdemeanour re-occur and when I telephoned the district office was told that it was my civic duty to split such objects in half. Paper side to one disposal unit, cardboard to the other.

I took my reprimand like a man and conscientiously followed the rules. However today saw a major slip-up. A

few weeks ago a circular arrived. A three-page gatefold and
a double-sided single sheet. Glossy paper, nicely printed in
eight colours. These were the NEW instructions as to dates
for putting out rubbish for collection. Most important was
that instead of Friday, our rubbish would be taken on
Monday. This information was also a News Item in the
parish magazine. I studied these documents with care and,
confident that my years at Oxford University had not been
wasted, we took five plastic sacks down the drive last night
and left them at the kerb side. We were especially glad to see
the back of them because I had missed the first new collection day and things were getting smelly. It's hot.

But this morning, setting off with my cleaner to dispose of
bottles, cans, newspapers, etc in the communal bins by the
Village Hall, what should I see but that my five bags of
malodorous rubbish were still there. Slight panic and mild
hysteria seized me. Finally, relatively calm, I phoned the
Council offices. A lengthy conversation revealed that I had
put the rubbish to be removed in the WRONG sort of
container. "We are only taking Food and Garden today,"
said the helpful girl. "But," I cried, "that is what it was."
"Ah, but in the wrong bags," she replied kindly, "You will
have to keep it now till next week."

So here I am on Midsummer's Day with five bags of stink-
ing rubbish. And six days to go. What to do? We can't leave
it outside, that would be fox heaven, it can't go in the greenhouse, that gets very hot indeed, it can't stay behind the
louvred doors outside the kitchen – we should all go down
with the plague. So we have locked it in the woodshed. The
woodshed gets hot and there is a broken window-pane, just
the way for a hungry fox to catch scent of a mega-feast. But
I have blocked off the broken pane with thick cardboard,
wedged in place with heavy logs. I figure this should defeat

Reynard. What really worries me is what will we find when we open up next Sunday, to take this ghastly pile of refuse to the kerb side? I have a nasty feeling that the smelly sacks in the woodshed may just stroll down the drive of their own accord.

XXVII

Perfection

29 June 2010

I woke up to that beautiful rarity – the perfect English summer morning. I'm not usually a one for dawn, but six o'clock today found me looking out of my bedroom window. A fine mist was rising off the water-meadows as the sun began to pull the damp out of the ground and the garden was awash with roses. The birds were about – a distant cuckoo called, rooks on the lawn pecked up bugs, pigeons scuffled in the beech trees, tiny wrens zipped back and forth, fat blackbirds sang and high above wheeled squealing house martins. The church clock chimed the quarter into a blue and cloudless sky. No other sounds and already the smell of grass and warm earth in the air. It doesn't get better than that.

For once everything an Englishwoman hopes for when she abandons the city and makes for the hills is all right here and has indeed been here this whole weekend. On Friday night we went for dinner with friends about thirty minutes from here, a pre-event for the main event, the hostess's husband's ninetieth birthday party. We stood out on the lawn, white wine in hand, gazing over acres of lush Cotswold countryside. I found myself chatting with a clergyman, recently retired, who was, on Sunday, to present a pageant on the story of Noah. He and his wife, he told me, drive about the county, their animals in a trailer behind them and present suitably themed pieces for important occasions. Book early for St Francis' Day! Was I in a P.G. Wodehouse novel or not?

Then on Saturday old and loved friends from America arrived. We sat in the dining room, a vast bowl of garden flowers on the table, the night air coming in from wide open windows, talking and laughing till one in the morning – and, that late, it was still balmy with a huge hanging moon.

Sunday brought another day of sun. After two hours with the hosepipe I changed into a light and frivolous frock and away we went for a 40th Wedding Anniversary lunch. Just an hour's drive and there we were – the happy couple, their best man, their bridesmaids, children, grandchildren and dear friends – seated in an open-sided marquee, not just so the air could move but also to show the boundless acreage of Northamptonshire stretching away and a somnolent group of Longhorn cattle lying below the ha-ha. Had everyone not been so happy this time I could have been in one of Thomas Hardy's pastorals. Drink flowed, conversation bubbled, heaped bowls of strawberries were so lustrously red they hardly seemed real.

Then home again, where our friends had just returned from a long day of garden and church viewing. A rest was in order. Then a drink on the terrace to hear their account of things seen and discovered. We stayed out on the terrace for dinner, candle flames upright in the still air, night-scented stocks spilling perfume and again a high fat moon turning the high trees into black cutouts against the night sky.

Three picture-perfect days in the heart of England. Blake's green and pleasant land was a joy to the eye and the soul.

These are hard times, but in truth this morning I had to agree with Robert Browning, "God's in His Heaven, All's right with the world".

XXVIII

Town Mouse, Country Mouse?

6 July 2010

Yesterday morning, Monday, I had to be up early. The builder/painter team was coming to the London flat, arrival time 8:00 am sharp. It had taken me until 11:20 pm on Sunday to finish stashing everything away, but nonetheless I was wide awake by 6:30 am, tackling the few last minute odds and ends before moving the car to a parking meter. This turned out to be a Good Thing – the team was early.

Everything we needed to discuss before they got started – paint colours, a couple of extra tasks – was sorted by 8:30 am. I was free to go. But where? I had an errand in the middle of town, but the store didn't open till 9:30 am. There was an hour to kill. So I drove down to Cavendish Square, put the car in the underground car park, bought myself a coffee and sat in the square.

I had a great time. Two Indian guys were sitting on the grass, not quite out of reach of the big lawn-sprinkler, giggling every time they got a slight shower, a black girl was doing her hair and makeup, coffee at her side, an older guy was on his cell phone, making obviously Important Calls, a fat lady of later years was studying what looked like medical notes. The world and its wife walked by. There was

a girl in exercise kit, another in full cocktail outfit, including high golden shoes and perfect maquillage, another, very
broad in the beam, carried a bulging file of papers – and the
men – short sleeves, long sleeves, business suits, briefcases,
dress-down office gear, cell-phones active or cell phones
clasped in readiness. Then there were a couple of dog-
walkers and a woman with a baby in a stroller. I saw more
people in half an hour than I would if I sat in Kempsford
High Street for a whole day. Buses, taxis, working-men in
vans drove by, bike-riders were present in swarms. "God,"
I thought, "this is wonderful! This is a city, full of life and
bustle, people! I should be HERE!"

Then, my errand done, I could drive home. I knew what
was waiting for me – watering, my grandson Freddie's toys
all over the nursery floor, serious thoughts on the future of
the Village Hall. Metropolitan life faded with each mile. "I
must be mad," I thought, "why am I heading for rural
stupor?"

But then I got here. And, as well as the tasks, all the things
I love were right under my nose. Broad beans ripe for
picking, lettuces ready to pull, roses right left and centre. I
cast aside my London outfit, shrugged into country-
bumpkin T-shirt and pedal-pushers, poured a large glass of
white wine and set lunch on the scrubbed pine of the
kitchen table. Outside it was very hot, but the tiled floor of
the kitchen was cool. A new literary journal had arrived in
the mail. After lunch I could sit under the sun umbrella and
read it in peace. Maybe this was the life after all?

Lunch was exceptionally delicious. Artichoke hearts, cold
roasted peppers and veg, Parma ham, really good bread –
all bought in London and ferried home, the best of both
worlds. Town mouse, country mouse? I guess I am half and
half.

XXIX

A Helluva Big Deal!

20 July 2010

For the next five days this small village becomes the centre of the universe. About two hundred thousand people will descend on it, with caravans, camper-vans, tents, SUVs, small cars, large cars, cameras, picnic baskets, flasks and, omnipresent, high-powered binoculars. The Royal International Air Tattoo is about to begin.

It has been taking place here for the last twenty-four years. Why? About ten minutes walk from our house is the longest Pentagon owned runway in Europe, at RAF Fairford. These days it is home to 420th Air Base Squadron and the Base Commander is a member of the USAF, but it started life as a major site for British air power in the 2nd World War. It is about to be mothballed – perhaps more of that anon, but the Tattoo is sacrosanct.

The last five years have raised over £1.5million for the RAF Charitable Trust. Beneficiaries under that umbrella include ex-servicemen, widows, the Girls' Venture Corps, Flying Scholarships for the Disabled, as well as other RAF stations which get help with improving social and welfare conditions. It is a real money-spinner.

However another reason for locals to put up with this

huge dislocation of everyday life is the vast amount of money it generates right here. Farmers turn their fields into parking lots, small landowners advertise camping facilities or Park and View sites, home-owners offer B&B, (one woman, no longer in the village, used to sleep under her dining-room table so as to free up her bedroom!). And the pub rakes it in, as do others close by. Last year local Tattoo set-up expenditure was £1,650,000. The Tattoo's donations to worthy causes are substantial and it creates extra employment opportunities.

So we hunker down and endure it. I make sure that there is nothing we need that we haven't got – it's six minutes in the car usually to my local shop. When the Tattoo is in full swing it can take forty, even with a RESIDENT sticker I have to go round the one-way system. So the cars stay in the garage. Only venues within walking distance can be considered – usually one neighbour or another will throw a barbecue or we might wander up to the perimeter fence to take a look at the planes.

This year's big aircraft attractions are the F22 Raptor and the debut of the RAF's new Airbus A400M. I don't think I care about either of them. However 2010 is the 70th anniversary of the Battle of Britain, so ancient planes will have dogfights, fly in the special "missing man" formation and there is to be an international flypast in salute to "The Few." As a war-baby whose Dad was in the RAF I guess I will be watching that.

The best bit of all will be the Red Arrows. As this team of fighters fly above at practically wing-tip distance from one another, leaving trails of red, white and blue behind them, you would have to have a heart of stone not to be astonished by both the pilots' skill and the grace of their wheeling acrobatics. An old and much-loved lady died here last week.

Her funeral is timed so that as she is lowered into the earth the Red Arrows will be rehearsing their flypast. What a way to go!

XXX

Hidden Treasures

27 July 2010

After thirteen years this village still springs surprises. I thought by now I knew its secrets – but no, the past few days have revealed two more. One is a computer company and the other a miracle-working garage.

We need the garage badly. In the wonderful way of the pre-occupied male my husband mashed up the car on our driveway wall. It's a Mercedes Estate and, were I to take it to a Mercedes specialist, I would be in for new strip, new door, new offside panel and re-spray – i.e. a Big Bill. Not a happy thought. Yesterday I was moaning to Monday's garden girl and she said cheerfully, "You need Dave Griffin." "Who's he?" I asked. "Go to the egg farm, drive in, eggs to the right, body-shop to the left." So I went.

Tucked away off the road is a modern bungalow, with a neat sign: "Free-Range Eggs." There are indeed eggs, but there is also a well-equipped garage and a handsome young man. He looked at the bruised motor with sympathy. Lip quivering I asked, "Can you fix it?" "No problem," says he. So I have a date – "Leave it here Sunday evening, put the keys through the letter-box and pick it up on Tuesday." I also have an estimate which will allow me to replenish the wine-cellar without selling the silver. If only I'd known

about him before! We are terrible bumpers into things and
have probably paid for a few mechanics' holidays – but that
is going to change. From now on I shall be off to the egg
farm whenever something needs fixing. I mentioned my
discovery to today's gardener – "Oh yes," he said, "he's
good."

Why has it taken me thirteen years to find him? Maybe
people in Big Houses are excluded from the village underground? I don't know and I don't care. Now I am in on this
secret for life!

As I made this magic connection my husband walked
down the village to the computer whizz. It's a small, semi-
detached house. Entry is through the kitchen's bachelor
chaos, a friendly dog escorts you upstairs and suddenly
wham, – it's the 21st century. Four large computer screens,
endless peripheral equipment and three guys. This is
Designtoo.

My husband wants them to set up his latest endeavour –
200 pages of descriptions of rare and unusual C18 poetry,
ranging from folio volumes to tiny pamphlets. Photographs
for illustrations are done, now the typeface and spacing
need agreeing. Then off to the printer – electronically. The
young boss can't understand why print needs to enter the
process at all. "Not necessary these days," he says, "I just
set you up a web-page with Links and the world's your
market place." Being old-fashioned my husband wants
print. But he has gone to see just what can be done. If it's
convincing enough – and why not? – maybe after 45 years
he'll change his ways. And the young man who can explain
it all is on the doorstep. But unless you're in the know you'd
never guess.

So this sleepy place holds two thriving independent businesses. Right now we hear endlessly from our government

about broken Britain, where state feather-bedding of the idle impoverishes us all. Not round here it doesn't, unless help is needed, when it's given. But slash, burn and tax is the name of the coalition's economic game. How will these two guys manage when VAT shoots up next year and people's pockets are even thinner? There is imagination and hard work tucked away here – but the small guys go under first. I hope I haven't discovered these two secrets just before they are wiped out. I'll let you know.

XXXI

My Vegetable Love

3 August 2010

I was born in a castle in Derbyshire, more by luck than judgement. After my natal day I missed out on country living, but all the while, on Parisian boulevards or Italian promenades, in Manhattan's canyons and on London's broad streets, I knew, deep down, that the country was where I belonged. I am an Englishwoman. The peak of my dreams is the wide lawn, the herbaceous border and the witty conversation over the dinner table. Said dinner of course enhanced by home-grown veg. From plot to plate.

However, after this summer's dry, dry weather I am beginning to wonder whether a nice caravan surrounded by asphalt might not prove more fertile ground, at least for conversation. Conversation presupposes reading, thought. But now the vegetables require watering. Watering requires time and the veg need it badly. Without water they become limp, sad, frail reproaches to their chatelaine. But with water – oh my – how they do provide.

"My vegetable love should grow
Vaster than empires"

wrote Andrew Marvell. I wonder whether he had actually

witnessed the ferocious production of a well-watered bed of
zucchini, or a similarly watered tub of runner beans or that
of a nicely moist couple of lines of beets and carrots. I
somehow think not. To promise that love would grow at
such a rate would have been quite daring. No room at all
for the odd tiff or slight estrangement – just ever-expanding
passion.

For how they do grow. Runner beans you can blanch and
freeze, carrots too, with beets you can make borscht and
whack it in the freezer. But zucchini multiply and the only
thing you can do is give them away, or spend hours making
freezable ratatouille, or give your husband grounds for
divorce by serving them nightly. I thought the only thing I
could hear in the night was this house's roof eating money,
but I was wrong. Now I hear the stealthy rustling of the
ever-expanding zucchini vines.

And I am not alone. It's hard to give away your zucchini
when everyone else is doing the same. The sophisticated
chat of the country dinner table is now entirely concen-
trated on the superfluity of veg and what to do with it. The
Game Fair passed us by, so did the first polo match of the
season. We are all war babies round here and know that
waste is wicked – somehow this glut must be accommo-
dated.

Fortunately Harvest Festival will take care of a lot, the
Village Fête will similarly require supplies. I have been to
our local bookstore, mostly stockist of light romance,
Gloucestershire history, gardening books and a few
provocative new novels. I have asked them to order me an
Italian cookery book that will tell me how properly to fry
zucchini flowers. That way I can stop the flow, produce
wonderful food and make my neighbours green with envy
because they didn't do the same.

For another quintessential element of English country life is competition. Unspoken, but rife. Whose crop is the tallest, whose horse has jumped highest? Soft-spoken competition exists in every area. But I feel confident – the secret killer recipe is en route – and I shall, just casually, say: "Well, do you think Andrew Marvell had ever seen a zucchini?"

XXXII

A Knotty Problem

10 August 2010

Some weeks back I mentioned Japanese Knotweed. *The Millbrook Independent*'s editor struck out this reference. He had never heard of it and thought that probably none of his readers would have either. But this week it is in the news here Big Time. "Fears over knotweed invasion" is *The Wiltshire and Gloucestershire Standard*'s banner headline.

It is a fiendish plant. Its stems are tall and rather resemble a bamboo. In the fall it produces delightful white flowers amidst lush green heart-shaped leaves. First introduced by the Victorians as a wonderfully decorative addition to the border, it now strikes fear and dread into the gardener's heart. You cannot get rid of it.

It has been found in an extensive development site on the outskirts of Cirencester, where new and badly-needed homes are being built. Unfortunately Japanese Knotweed can cheerfully grow through foundations, tennis courts and highways. It brings down walls. More than £150 million is spent in the UK annually by the Environment Agency on knotweed control. By law landowners must be proactive in its eradication. All parts of the plant are classified as controlled waste and must be removed and disposed of by a licensed waste control operator. It can grow up to 10cm a day. Its roots can dig three metres into the soil and spread as much as seven metres from the plant. It prevents the growth of other natural vegetation. A county councillor has described it as "One of the most evil natural things that could happen to the town."

I know what to do with it in the garden. I cut it at about a foot above ground and with an eye-dropper put weed-killer into the hollow stem. This gets into the roots and eventually kills it. It is a very time-consuming procedure, but worth it. I however am dealing with one big herbaceous border. The panic now on the construction site rests mainly on the effect the mandatory removal of the plant and the earth in which it is growing will have on the costs of the homes due to spring up in its place.

The UK is in urgent need of more housing stock and a development such as that now under attack from this wretched plant is seen as an essential investment in local life. The landowner is responsible for tackling the invasion. But who is the landowner? The construction company? It will certainly not have built the cost of disposing of polluted soil into its calculations of the final purchase price of the homes. Or perhaps the land is long-leased from the original landowner who will now need to foot a bill he had no idea of when doing the deal with the builders. Either way it is going to be a headache of major proportions.

But whoever ends up in the financial hot seat, one thing is clear. The houses will be a long time in coming and they will be very expensive. Possibly the only benefit from this unexpected hazard will be that double dip recession, should it, as is suggested, appear, will be long gone. We took the American grandchildren today to see some of the astonishing Roman mosaics found here in the nineteenth century. One can only hope that the houses currently meant to be ready for occupation in the spring/summer of 2011 will not be similar marvels of antiquity when they are at last completed.

XXXIII

The Wasp Man Cometh

17 August 2010

Bees are one thing, wasps another. We have two bee colonies living here, ensconced in the old lathe and plaster wall-linings, entry through the Cotswold stone roof. They are close neighbours, yet we have no territorial problems. We have got used to them and in view of the worry of declining bee numbers are rather proud to be giving them house room. They bumble busily round the lavenders, roses and buddleias, doing us no harm.

But we have also become a five star wasp destination, with three independent nests at the back of the house. One entry is just above my study. I was typing one day and became aware of a strange scrabbly little noise. Right over my desk are two old beams and they were the sound's source. "Ohmigod," I thought, "Death-watch beetle. The house will fall down." Investigation revealed that that was not so – looking up from the terrace I could see a constant stream of wasps, sneaking in under a tile. My overhead beam was a serious wasps' hang-out. While gazing up at the spot I realised another stream of black and yellow stripes was making for a hole maybe six feet distant and that this lot were sneaking into the roof under a lead flashing in the adjacent gable. Not a happy sight. Then, going down from the terrace, I saw yet another constant flow of winged stingers. Right in the steps down to the lawn and this seemed to be the busiest venue of the lot. As I suffer from anaphylactic shock and one sting could finish me, I felt there was a message here. And the message was "Call the Wasp Man." So I did. And today he came.

For lunch with visitors we had to sit on the far side of the house by the vegetable garden. Even so the fliers found us and it was constant wasp alert. Not good for the nerves! But as our guests left, the Wasp Man arrived.

Even though a hardened professional he seemed quite impressed by our collection. But unfazed. "Close the windows and the doors this side," he said, "and leave it to me. I wouldn't come out here till morning – there'll be a lot of wasps hanging around." Then donning protective hat and mask he got to work. He attached a long extending pipe to a huge plastic spray tub, pointed the nozzle at the end of the pipe into the entries to the nests and then pushed and pulled on the tub's plunger. A cloud of white dust emerged and I left him to it.

About ten minutes later he appeared at the kitchen door. "Right," he said, "that should do it. That'll be £90. If you have a problem get in touch." Then he drove away.

I went upstairs to look out and see what was happening. Thousands of wasps were winging and circling, some going into the nests, some coming out. The air was seething. It was a horrible sight. And not just because they were wasps. It was something to do with the numbers. Some years back we flew low over Namibia's coast to see the seal colonies. I love seals, playful, intelligent, beautiful. But seeing about a million of them wriggling and squiggling and glistening in the sun was quite stomach-turning. No longer individual they became an alien life-swarm.

Why? Because they were part of the structure of the life of the planet? One to which I had no link, nor any understanding of their obviously complex lives? Or that the strength of the natural world was so vividly displayed? Perhaps. It can't just have been the numbers – wasps or seals – because I don't feel that way when I gaze up on a summer's night and see the heavens teeming with stars.

XXXIV

Nature's Way

24 August 2010

The drought is over. Round here it has been coming down in sheets – and I can't say I'm sorry. Nor is anybody else. Farmers are OK – they have got their crops in. Last week the roar of harvesters was everywhere. Huge round bales stood in the fields waiting for collection and every local road was either taken over by a slow tractor pulling a trailer loaded high or covered in a layer of straw fallen off in transit. Far from being a peaceful countryside retreat the village became a hub of agricultural activity. Growers looked cheerful. They looked particularly cheerful because, thanks to the shocking fires in Russia the price of wheat, which had been pretty much rock bottom, has risen to a respectable number.

Gardens are also reviving. Our lawns looked like Abu Dhabi, but now they are greening up nicely and this week I may actually ask the gardener to get the mowers out. Tomorrow a local lad comes for a few hours in the morning and I shall have him up a ladder unblocking gutters. Stuffed up with debris gone solid under the continuous sun they have been cascading down like mini Niagaras. Water from its traditional source is once again part of our lives. Though not yet stowed away for winter the hoses lie coiled, rather than snaked out over the ground because it wasn't worth tidying them up when you'd be out again for three hours the next evening. The kitchen garden water butt is full too, so now you can just dunk in a watering-can to do the greenhouse tomatoes, peppers and aubergines. Everyone is happy.

How different for us than for those in Pakistan. I thought that tonight especially. We have a ditch, maybe eight feet deep, running along the top of the bottom paddock. It takes water from a spring into the Thames. It has been so dry this year that it had become completely stuffed with reeds, yellow water flags, nettles, perfect cover for horse-flies and mosquitoes to breed and breed. So ten days ago a man came with a digger and dredger to clean it out. It took him two days and we were left with an empty trench, just a bit muddy at the bottom. Indeed it was so tempting a sight that six year old Freddie decided to walk along it – and lost one of his wellies in the sludge!

I just went down to check it out. The water is five feet deep and three feet across after the past two days of heavy downpours. The pressure from the river water is now so strong it is pushing water back up our inlet. Yet all summer the river level has been barely high enough to take a canoe. This has happened FAST.

How terrifying to watch water rise and rise and rise. To see it consuming your home, your land, your life. It won't happen to us until the whole of Wiltshire is under water – we are fourteen feet higher than the fields we look out on. But the past few days have been a quite salutary reminder that Nature is not necessarily benign and that for all our know-how we are still at the mercy of the uncontrollable.

XXXV

The Ties that Bind

31 August 2010

It's over! August Bank Holiday, the English Labour Day, is done and dusted. Saturday, Sunday, Monday – free time for all – then back to the grind. Summer has been officially closed. And, mirabile dictu, on Thursday it's back to school.

This past Thursday we went to London – my husband and my daughter to watch the first day of the Test Match – and me to keep young Freddie busy. We left them at Lords Cricket Ground and set forth. Every possible child-interesting venue was mobbed. At Madame Tussaud's the queue just to buy a ticket was a two-hour wait – the Science Museum line went round the block, as did that at the Museum of Natural History. Exhausted grandparents and parents, surrounded by vociferous children, looked about as cheerful as a man waiting to be hanged.

Now it's finished. But it has made me think. This weekend we had Freddie here, because his mother was filming, but an old friend too, who looked after his mum for me when she was just about his age. A couple of weekends back we had my nephew from Australia along with a young man who was at university with my daughter. We were thrilled to see them. One was a blood relation and the other a true friend. In between these two visits I have dealt with a cousin and family and also one of my sisters and her family. None of these experiences has been disagreeable, but all have been exhausting. You can't say no to your family, blood is blood. But the pleasure of entertaining people from your past is quite another story.

Reflecting on this sequence of visitors who needed to be fed and watered, I wondered just what are the ties that bind? For children and grandchildren you are on auto cue – but there's another range of choice. People you have known forever, people who were there at a big moment in your life, people you love, people to whom, for whatever reason, you feel you owe a duty of care. These are the ties you cannot escape. They have come from your life, your personal narrative.

If push came to shove I would, except for my daughter and grandson, give the family the old heave-ho. The ties that really bind are, for me, shared experience, shared frames of reference, shared convictions. Nothing much to do with people I ought to love, but mostly just put up with because that's what you do.

The big Cotswold moment for me this weekend was planting some small box trees round the base of a newly-installed memorial tablet to my parents. Their mingled ashes are in a sandalwood box that was on our mantelpiece for years, set beneath a flagstaff I have had erected in our churchyard. The person who helped me dig the planting trench and put in the bonemeal compost was not a family member, but my friend of nearly forty years.

She loves plants and so do I. I knew she would enjoy that digging and setting of shrubs and I knew too she would like to be a part of this, my final farewell. Our shared concerns go back a long way. Those are the ties that bind.

XXXVI

The Fête Worse than Death

7 September 2010

It's Autumn. The last blast of Game Fairs, Village Shows, Ploughing Competitions and Steam Rallies is in full swing, Cotswolds-wide. But the fêtes reign supreme. Almost every turn on the road from Kempsford to Cirencester has a hand-lettered sign in the verge, pointing toward the Northleach, Eastleach, Southrop, Ampney Crucis Church Fêtes. And this weekend we had ours.

Always at the Manor, always vintage cars, always a raffle, always a dog show, always a bottle stall, always the Vicar keeping the show on the road, hanging out with his flock. And always a plant stall. There may be havoc in far-flung places, there may be serious questions of icecaps melting, or indeed a Parliamentary scandal brewing – but nothing comes between a village and its Fête.

In the morning the High Street is busy with helpers converging to set up stalls, arrange tea-tables (no Fête can be held without tea and cakes), or organize seating for the Chedworth Silver Band. By two o'clock all is in order. The fun can begin.

But where exactly is the fun? Not perhaps in the usual mega clear-out of toys, ladies' no-longer fashionable gear, books read and not required and CDs and tapes of once not-to-be-missed bands. Plus objects too ghastly to be worthy of further shelter in the happy home. A glorified Boot Sale, with music and tea on the side. Total takings with luck £2,500.

But the fun... there is the guy who last year had quite a different girlfriend. There is the horrible child who regularly throws up on the lawn. There is the widow now looking chirpy, there is the man you have avoided all year, but whom you must now cheerfully greet. There are the lady Morris dancers who should have been interred en route so doleful is their demeanour. And there's winning the raffle, picking a lucky ticket at the bottle stall (for something you don't like!) – and watching everybody being busy.

And there is the GOSSIP. Did you know, someone asks me, X's wife is now shacking up with Y? I did not. As X is a poor fellow with only one arm and one leg due to a fearful accident and Y is a man whose wife is lost to Alzheimer's this is an intriguing tale. What do the adulterous couple chat about in the evenings? Did you know, asks another, SoandSo is booked in for plastic surgery? "Did you know?" or "Have you heard?" prefaces the scuttlebutt of a small community and I would never hear it if I were not at the Fête. I love it.

The goods on offer cannot compare with the grandeur of those for auction in Millbrook. American Hepplewhite and Chippendale furniture, polo mallets, top hats, Tang ceramics – just some of the St Peter's fund-raising possibilities. But the sheer lunacy of this endeavour, coupled with the participants' faith that it is worth doing, makes it an event not to be missed. Ritual is all. Stephen Hawking explained last week why, quite definitely, God does not exist. He is probably right. But Kempsford's church does and the Fête will help keep it standing for a bit longer. And the broad church that is village life is sustained too, because this is what, once a year, we do. As Joyce Grenfell so perfectly put it, it is the Fête worse than death – but, if we keep on going: "Oh Death, where is thy sting?"

XXXVII

We Will Remember Them

21 September 2010

Since the last despatch your Cotswold Correspondent has been on holiday. Just a hop and a skip across the Channel, first to Normandy and then to Italy. Both stopovers were with American friends who had chosen Europe for this year's vacation. What a debt of gratitude we owe them. Not only for their hospitality, but also because they reminded us just how close Europe is and how wonderful. These days one tends to associate vacations with long-haul flights to far-flung places, but three hours away, on Eurostar, with a quick change in Paris, are the delights of oysters, langoustines, merlin and lobster. Not to mention the rich variety of traditional Calvadossian fare – pâtés, terrines, cider, Camembert – fresh, fresh and local.

And when you have had enough, you get on the train again. To Porto Ercole, close to Rome, where pasta, risotto, funghi porcini, fritto misto and saltimbocca wreak further havoc on the waist-line. But the churches, the paintings, the sea, the colours, all play their part in making you feel you are ABROAD. Everything is fairly familiar, no little boys rush up to you to try to clean your shoes while you are walking, no astonishingly able tailor will knock you up a suit or a ball-gown for the price of a candy-bar, the exotic and the dangerous are not part of the holiday frame. But it is different enough to be refreshing, stimulating and fun. Nor do you need to feel guilty because you are so much richer than the people whose country you are visiting.

That is a big change. When I was a girl, travelling with my parents, Europe was still in post-war recovery mode and people were poor. You did NOT drink the water out of the tap and you kept your pocket-book under close watch at all times. These days, even with the present global economic problems, you and the folk you are mixing with are pretty much even. That is relaxing.

While we were in Normandy we went to pay our respects at the American Cemetery and Memorial. You look down on Omaha Beach amidst a forest of white crosses and Stars of David, each commemorating a life lost. There is a Garden of the Missing too, laid out with beds of polyantha roses beneath tablets engraved for those whose bodies were never found. It was busy, families were still coming to visit their dead, others to see for real what so many movies have portrayed. The unwavering marble lines of remembrance high above the beaches say it all.

This summer was the 70th anniversary of the Battle of Britain and there has been a wave of national remembrance and gratitude for the unbelievable bravery both of the RAF and the civilian population. Those who were alive then are now either dead or pretty old – I am not sure how much the grainy black and white newsreels mean to the young. It must be somewhat similar in the US. The great generals and leaders are long gone – the global frame of reference has changed. Sometimes now America and Europe are at loggerheads. But standing in Normandy in that quiet place you are incredibly grateful. For without the bravery of those soldiers – British, Canadian and American – delightful holidays such as I have just enjoyed would not be possible. Our happiness is their memorial.

XXXVIII

"Season of Mists and Mellow Fruitfulness"

28 September 2010

Inexorably the end of the year creeps up on us. Garden tidying becomes imperative. And, going through closets and chests of drawers to exhume the winter warmers, the standard autumn questions arise – have the mothballs worked? Can I still fit into these garments? But there's one joyous marker buoy – Harvest Festival.

It is a wonderful celebration. I loved it as a London child and I love it even more now that my study window looks out over fields where all is indeed safely gathered in. And from where earlier in the year I have watched the ploughing and the scattering. The early Church absorbed many pagan festivals, turning their ancient timing into occasions suitable for the Christian calendar. Celebration of the harvest is one that didn't require a makeover. Harvest achieved is harvest achieved to whatever deity you subscribe.

Kempsford church was decked out to the nines. Hydrangeas, pink roses, Michaelmas daisies and garlands filled the porch, the font was surrounded by sunflowers, hawthorn and grasses. By the vestry door, sedums and chrysanthemums glowed. The pulpit was wreathed in garlands, ivy, monarda, golden rod and dahlias. Pyracantha, sedums and gladioli were at the base of the tower, while ivy, hawthorn and crab-apple adorned the entry to the choir.

But there were no vegetables, no corn stooks and no huge loaves of bread woven into a harvest braid. Times are changing. When I was a child the mega-marrows, cabbages, tomatoes and baskets of apples were indispensable. Back then after the harvest service these fresh vegetables and fruits were taken immediately to the local hospital, or orphanage, or old folks' home. In today's better-off society the giving is no less generous, but the end destination differs. As do the gifts. These are destined for the Red Cross, Oxfam, Save the Children – charities that fly help and relief all over the world when crisis strikes. So the candles shine down on coffee packs, rice packs and tins – of tuna, noodles, corn, peaches, baked beans, pilchards, soup, rice pudding, tomatoes – and on tea-bags, long-life fruit juice, bottled olive oil, breakfast cereal, pasta. Not as beautiful as in the old days, but as nourishing and as needed.

One of the Readings was from 2 Corinthians 9: 6-11, "God loveth a cheerful giver." Being a cheerful giver is something open to pretty much everyone nowadays. Especially at this festival. Harvest is the time, but the fruits of the earth are no longer the way to go. Much that was given had been bought at the supermarket. But it was food and destined for those truly in need. And to make these somewhat everyday offerings appropriately festive they came in decorated parcels – some in silver paper, some in brown, with birds' feathers glued to them, others sported children's drawings and lettering. Cheerful offerings indeed.

After the service it was back to a Harvest Festival lunch at the pub – some straw bales for the children to clamber on, good solid sandwiches to engage the grown-ups. A very village occasion and one where people's thoughts were, just briefly, directed collectively beyond their immediate frame of reference. They were, as 1 Chronicles 29: 9 puts it, rejoicing "for that they offered willingly ... with perfect heart". Truly a heart-warming Autumn moment.

XXXIX

"What a Tangled Web"

5 October 2010

We have had spiders on the brain in this house this week. My poor husband came back from our Italian idyll with three spider bites that suddenly got the better of his immune system, so rather than being itchy annoyances they became huge red, hot, hard blobs. Antibiotics are doing the trick, but these blobs are nasty. Spiders are also everywhere in the house – you could knit a jumper out of our cobwebs, they are so many and so thick. And every time you fancy a bath there is a hairy friend waiting for you. I am afraid I sluice them right back down their plughole entrance, despite being told by eco-sensitive friends that I should pick them up and put them out of the window. As for the garden – the webs are everywhere and on a sunny morning when the dew is still fresh the symmetry of their sparkling patterns glistens and amazes. The other day there was one gossamer thread going from a raspberry cane to a bean-pole – fifteen feet away – defying gravity. How does a spider do it? One can only marvel.

And yet the spider's web, so beautiful and astonishing, has become the synonym for wickedness, cunning, deception. We have read a lot about those nasty attributes in the newspapers this week. The new Leader of the Opposition bested his older brother in his party's vote and is therefore variously charged with fratricide, hubris and plot-weaving. The spider's web theory of internecine goings-on between high-level politicians has had a really good airing. Now the Conservatives, the Prime Minister's party, are holding their annual conference and the web theory is out again. I can quite see that politics is a game played on multiple levels – but why should spiders carry the can? Their only aim is to catch flies.

Then of course there's www. The worldwide web. We are all caught up in it, inter-connected by millions of invisible cyberspace threads. But it's not a proper web. The spider's web is an exquisitely precise creation, geometric, perfectly constructed into patterns of space, each little line of gossamer having a structural purpose. In my experience, typing www. onto the computer is a sure way to irritation, loss of focus and a deluge of unwanted information. You need a will of steel to fight your way through to find what you seek. And to ignore the endlessly annoying side-bars. A very poor web by spider standards.

It was Sir Walter Scott, in *Marmion* (1808) who wrote: "Oh what a tangled web we weave, when first we practise to deceive". I think he got it right. An honest man, he was seeking to define the endless troubles caused by deception. What better image than "a tangled web"? The beauty of the spider's web lies in the inexorable logic of its pattern. I have never seen a tangled one. But once you start to imagine all those little joints of gossamer heading the wrong way, what visual confusion that creates. How could it be unpicked and remade?

Tonight everyone is talking about the Chancellor of the Exchequer's plan to sort out the economy. Elsewhere in Europe politicians debate immigration, labour troubles, welfare dependency etc etc etc. One side of the argument presents the statistics in one way and the opposing forces in another. The web is tangled indeed.

As a conscientious citizen I must follow all these arguments and try to find a truth. It is quite tiring. But I shall feel better in the morning when I go out onto the lawn and see an ocean of perfect patterns under the sun.

XL

Brock the Badger – Best Friend or Bane?

12 October 2010

There can't be many people who haven't heard of *The Wind in the Willows* and its famous fellowship. Dreadful show-off Mr Toad, with his penchant for fast cars, delightfully urbane Ratty, whose picnics are delicious beyond belief and dear Moley, the quiet shy fellow, astonished to have acquired Ratty as a friend. And then of course there is Badger. Counsellor, sage and nemesis of the Weasels. Kenneth Grahame's classic children's tale still holds up in the twenty-first century. Summer sees it performed by Amateur Dramatic Societies the length and breadth of England and in the Christmas season it frequently hits the West End stage. Toad is the pantomime Dame, and Badger, always in his slightly worn smoking-jacket and slippers, the good genie.

Well, all this may work just fine as a kind of uber-saga for the young, but in real terms I'd rather have my toad in the cellars catching flies than my badger in his sett at the end of the garden. He rootles up newly placed plants and, in high summer, digs tracks that make the lawn look like a replay of the Battle of Arnhem, as he searches out succulent chafer grubs. Dairy farmers are not too keen on badgers either. It is highly likely that they transfer bovine TB, but a call for a substantial badger cull has provoked fierce argument. On 15 September this year government proposals for a Licence to Cull were outlined – last year bovine TB cost the country £63 million – but earlier this year the Court of Appeal quashed permission to cull in Wales. Definitely the jury is still out.

However badgers have been in the news in Kempsford for quite another reason. Badger damage to two village roads has been so bad that they have been closed for five days for Gloucestershire Highways Department to carry out repairs. Excavation of the setts is the first step and a vet must be on site in case any live animals are found in the process. Any such animals must be appropriately relocated. Repairs are also a complicated business since private properties close to the works affect access. In addition there are likely to be more badger runs. There are several gravel extraction sites on the outskirts of the village and that is probably where the badger vandals are getting a head start.

So the persona of Mr Badger, much-loved children's friend and literary icon, is taking a bit of a bashing round here. I was wondering whether there is another such graphic example of an animal personality swap. From friend to fiend – or vice versa. I could only think of dragons. They were fearful creatures, breathing fire and wreaking havoc. You wouldn't want a dragon in the neighbourhood. But then, hey presto, there was Puff the Magic Dragon and dragons were just the sweetest thing.

There is a huge Save the Badger movement here – and a quite substantial one to the contrary. But maybe *Wind in the Willows* can have the last word. As Badger says to Mole, "And now there are badgers here again. We are an enduring lot, and we may move out for a time, but we wait, and are patient, and back we come. And so it will ever be". Perhaps in these times of anxiety as to the planet's future we should see the invasion of the badger as a sign of hope. They will, as far as they are concerned, always be around.

XLI

Who's to Blame?

19 October 2010

Last week I had fun writing about badgers and their wicked ways. But *The Millbrook Independent*'s Editor felt that a more weighty matter, i.e. the upcoming mid-term elections, needed the space. He was of course right. Nothing is more important than who we choose to represent us.

So perhaps this week readers might like to know how things look from this side of the pond. It matters, especially in this house, since we are both US citizens – my husband by birth and me by choice. We follow matters carefully. It is easy to do, as the English media gives the topic extensive coverage.

Put at its most simple it looks to us as though the American electorate has gone barking mad. "I'm not a witch … I'm you", from one popular candidate and "I'm not a politician, I'm an accountant and a manufacturer", from another, and from yet another the fictitious nature of autism as a disease – leave out global warming being down to sunspots, or the mythical nature of evolution, forget the President's not really being a citizen – by far the most depressing feature is the fact that people will believe this rubbish.

This despite the fact that since the 2009 Inauguration America's moral standing in the rest of the world has been restored, that America is now in compliance with the Geneva Convention, that the financial system has been stabilized thanks to TARP, (February 2009), that the ReFi Programme of the same month has begun to create jobs by the renewal of national infrastructure and that the PPAC of 2010 is the most important piece of American social legislation since Lyndon Johnson's Health Care Bill of 1965.

What more do people want? It is not hard to see that unemployment figures remain alarming, but they could be worse; mortgage collapse is frightening, but full recession has been narrowly avoided; the decay of Main Street businesses is shocking, but a stabilized financial system makes recovery possible. A global financial meltdown left us all in the cart. Why is it hard to see that recovery, shaky but there, has been given breath by the current Administration?

We were talking about this yesterday. As you will have gathered this is a fairly liberal household. We had guests of a more right-leaning nature. Our own government is about to put in place the most draconian Budget plans for over sixty years. They will without doubt cause immense problems, especially for people who are not very well off. But the country, at present, seems inclined to put up, shut up and suffer. Why? It has somehow been presented as entirely the previous government's fault that national finances are in disorder. No reference to global collapse is to be found. It has also been presented that a nation's budget must be run like that of the average home. A kind of self-induced hypnosis has taken over.

I wonder, when did we all forget to think? Or indeed when did we become SO lazy that we ceased to question our assumptions of what is due to us, or to try to understand the hard questions of plus and minus in the economic structures of our world. It is a lot easier to blame somebody else – with us the last government, with you the present Administration – than to sit down and think that perhaps we too played a role. We were all very happy to take the good times for granted, but did we ever think just how they came about? I think not and I'm as guilty as the next man.

What seems very clear is that now, more than ever, every last man-jack with the right to vote needs to ask proper questions and not be lulled into acceptance of the easy rather than the uncomfortable truth. Some of it, at least, was our own fault. The Tea Party Movement has been described as "A grass roots citizens' movement brought to you by a bunch of oil billionaires". Better for us all that rather than be part of a movement we should be an individual citizen. Good luck.

XLII

Halloween vs Guy Fawkes

26 October 2010

When I was a child Halloween didn't exist. We had plenty of other days for fun and at this time of year it was Guy Fawkes Day, or Bonfire Night, that occupied us. We made guys from old socks and pillowcases stuffed with rags and newspapers, then topped them off with a painted face and one of Dad's old hats before sitting in the street shouting, "Penny for the guy!" It was total fun. Occasionally some lucky children would get hold of a wheelbarrow and they would push their guys up and down the High Street, bellowing, "Penny for the guy!" to all. On 5 November we had bonfires in our back gardens, with Catherine Wheels and rockets and sparklers lighting up the night and, as a last rite before bed, we would put the guy on top of the fire and watch him go up in smoke. Then we could start concentrating on Christmas.

The first I heard of Halloween was at boarding school, when a couple of the older girls decided to dress up as witches and leap out on us young ones from dark corners. This made us scream, a favourite occupation of adolescent girls, and so, for us, the idea caught on and ghosts and witches became standard procedure on 31 October. But in the outside world Guy Fawkes continued supreme and he was still the big autumn attraction for my daughter.

Then, stealthily, Halloween crept in, partly because every year some truly gruesome accident or the death from fright of someone's much-loved pet would be graphically reported. Eventually government Health and Safety rules took over. Local councils organized communal bonfires and firework displays. Though often spectacular, they did rather take the individual out of the equation.

Just like Nature children abhor a vacuum and what better to fill the vacant space than Halloween? Dressing up, spooky ghosts, spiders and frightening friends and neighbours, all were sanctioned. And you got a chance to eat yourself sick with sweets from Trick or Treat knocks on local doors. Plus you could douse the lights and have supper in the eerie glow of the pumpkin lantern. What started life as a mediaeval celebration in remembrance of the dead slowly turned into a jolly occasion. Of course apple-bobbing and pranks between neighbours had always been part of the tradition, but for centuries All Hallows' Day and All Souls' Day were its heart.

Not much of that remains in folk-memory these days. And Health and Safety are once more involved. People have given children poisoned treats, some of the tricks require things more threatening than you'd like, children wandering the streets unsupervised make us anxious and some older kids have been casing the joint with an eye to burglary. All a bit depressing – and I have not even mentioned the commercialisation!

Fortunately this is a small place so there is little likelihood of harm. It is also extremely cold and the majority of children will be tucked up with their mobiles, sending terrifying pictures to one another, rather than prowling about in the frosty dark. Plus these days Harry Potter has pretty much cornered the ghost/witch/wizard market – you might almost describe ghosts as has-beens. But I will lay in a few bars of chocolate and a chewy toffee spider or two, plus a basket of tangerines. Then if the knocks on the door happen, we'll be prepared.

But I'll also have a few fireworks for 5 November. No need at all for one tradition to completely oust another. Especially when you are surrounded by spreading, empty autumn fields.